JUST THINKING
SPIRITUAL REFLECTIONS AND POETRY

DR. CHARLES A. GUILFORD, III

Copyright © 2021 Charles A. Guilford III

All rights reserved.

No part of this publication in print or in electronic format may be reproduced, stored in a retrieval system, or transmitted in any form or by any means, electronic, mechanical, photocopying, recording, or otherwise without the prior written permission of the publisher.

The scanning, uploading, and distribution of this book without permission is a theft of the author's intellectual property. If you would like permission to use material from the book (other than for review purposes), please contact drguilford@theteacherteacherllc.com. Thank you for your support of the author's rights.

Distributed by Bublish, Inc.
Paperback ISBN: 978-1-647043-38-4
eBook ISBN: 978-1-647043-37-7

Dedicated to my wife and son—my world.

TABLE OF CONTENTS

Preface xi
Guilty Gifts 1
Painful Understanding. 3
Park It 4
Stop Trying to Peek. 6
The Limp Limb. 8
Right Clothes, Wrong Cause 10
Change Ain't Comin'. 12
Shut Up 14
Silence 15
Skeletons in the Closet 16
God's Child Too 18
"I Ain't Got It!". 20
Sista Souljah 22
Another Woman 23
What Gives Us the Right? 24
Check It Out 26

- Who You Be? 27
- "Phone Check, Punk!". 28
- Money in the Bank 30
- The Antidote. 31
- My Father's Forehead 33
- Contempt. 35
- Treasure Chest 36
- And a Child Shall Lead Them 38
- Disciples Do Panic 40
- Listen, Listen 42
- Nothing to Give 43
- Our Right to Complain. 45
- You Don't Belong Here 47
- Can You See What I See?. 49
- The Role of the Wife. 51
- Silence on the Set 53
- The Message, Not the Messenger 54
- Attitude Adjustment 55
- Still Going 57
- Chain Reaction. 59
- Anonymous Angels 61
- His Eyes Are on You, Not Them 63
- Righteous or Perfection. 65
- Be Still 66

Free Time	68
More Than Enough	70
Be Encouraged	72
Be Ready to Pray	73
Can't Find Time? Make it	75
Temporary Residency	76
Praise, No Matter What	78
Repeat Offenders	80
Angels of Light?	82
Little Steps	84
Compassion	86
More Than Fans	88
Share the Struggle	90
Window Shopping	92
Let 'Em Talk	94
Our Self	96
The Dirty Room	98
Throw Some Wood on the Fire	99
Waiting in the Toolbox	100
Are You Willing to Wait?	102
Don't Speak About It, Be About It	103
Why Me, Lord?	105
A Blessing Not Earned	107
Good Advice	108

The Gift That Keeps Giving	109
Finally, I Cried	110
Training Day	112
Temptations	114
Faith Quiz	116
The Enemy We Hate to Love	117
Where Is the Fear?	118
Living the Life, or a Lifestyle?	120
An Enjoyer	122
Travel Plans	123
We Ain't Seeing Clearly	125
I Love God More	126
Don't Look Like No Saint	127
Sharing	128
Church Today?	130
Message for Me	131
Trying Times	133
Too Righteous?	134
Be Encouraged on This Day	136
Calorie Counting	138
Confirmation	139
God Loves You	140
Feeling or Faith?	141
Got Patience?	142

Mercy	143
Stress?	144
One Day at a Time	145
A Moment	146
Power	147
Poetry	149
All in the Letter	151
Approaching Fast	153
Church Announcements	155
Commands for the Future	159
Hate On, World	161
Her Rewards	163
Like Solomon Prayed	165
Loved and Chastened	167
No Serpent for Me	169
Remaining the Same	171
The Healing of Sliders	173
The Second Delivery	175
Thing Seeker	176
This Morning	178
Timothy's Example	180
Who Do We Call?	182
Author Bio	185

PREFACE

I am not a pastor, preacher, or prophet. I have no schooling in divinity. I share this in the preface so that there is no confusion, delusion, or perceived misrepresentation. The words, thoughts, and ideas that follow are simply that—just my thoughts. Originating as a daily email thread, these thoughts have been compiled in a collection and combined with relevant poetic creations. They are derived from experiences, ponderings, meditations, periods of solitude, and biblical reflections. Their creation was therapeutic for me. I hope all will find something worthwhile in these pages.

Dr. Guilford (2021)

Guilty Gifts

A church patron gives tithes out of obligation. A drug dealer sells poison to the community, but then gives food to the homeless. A husband abuses his wife, and then buys her jewelry and flowers. Or how 'bout this? A person gives a stranger money with the greedy intent of getting it returned to him tenfold. I love how God works! He considers the act, but also looks at the motive (1 Chron. 28:9). Humans see the act itself and are awed by the gestures, but God—oh, God gets to the source. Sometimes we do a good thing for all the wrong reasons. I have found myself giving my time, my energy, and even my money at times, but I do not always stop to consider my motives. The examples given show that ulterior motives cause my actions to become hypocrisy. Why? God's Word states that we should do things out of love, without any expectation of anything back (Luke 6:35). This includes doing things out of guilt as well. Confession time! Once, I did not get my wife a gift for our anniversary, and when it became an issue, I immediately ran out and got one. Needless to say, it was not accepted. She did not want a gift that was offered out of guilt—she wanted one offered with love. God sets our standards high, and all we can do is try. Be mindful of why we do things, because just like the drug dealer, the husband, the stranger, and the church patron, our actions may be motivated by something other than love. Is what counts that which we are doing or why we are doing it? Only you and God know!

Just thinking.

Painful Understanding

They say a wise man learns from the mistakes of others. Well, with that understanding, I appreciate the children of Israel. Psalm 78:29–33 talks about how God provided them with their own desires (not needs, but desires), then He sent His wrath, and after all that they still sinned and did not believe in the ability of God (Ps. 78:32). Okay, let me get this straight. God showed them how kind and how angry He could be, and they still did not believe? As the old folks say, "They must have been *touched*." But back to the wise man. Can we see the error here? God shows us what we need to see and teaches us the lessons we need to learn, hoping we willingly change. But that was not the case for the children of Israel. I have found myself in awe of God's glory at times, and still in disbelief like the children of Israel. Honestly, I'm tired of the painful lessons. I seek now to learn from a distance as much as I can, and I hope the lessons learned from others limit my mistakes. I will make enough mistakes on my own. I don't need to repeat the failures of others, do I? God is God. He ain't changin'! He will continue to teach. It all depends on what type of teaching we require!

Just thinking.

Park It

There are songs about the "secret place" (and even the old folks talk about it). This refers to the place in which you are secluded in the presence of God and not distracted by the outside world (Ps. 91). You are at peace and can focus on God and His glory. You can talk, pray, give thanks, and praise as loudly and as often as you like. The "secret place"! I have a secret place. If you are like me, finding a place at home is often impossible! LOL. Not that you can't, but it is tough. I usually have to wait for everyone to go to sleep before getting that type of peace. But when I really need to go to my secret place, I go to the park. Any *safe park*! LOL. During the day, I am blessed with aerial scenery you would not believe. A landscape that is remarkable, animals moving through the day, and quiet—oh, how quiet it is. Not only does the park provide a time to speak with the Lord, but it also helps me to appreciate Him. He created all that I have described (Gen. 1:21). Nature is beautiful, and when you take time to really sit and appreciate it, you develop a greater appreciation for God. Today, things move fast, and taking time out is more important than ever. We need that peace and quiet in order to gather our thoughts and to talk with the Lord. If you have a secret place, go now! If you don't, try the safe park (I stress *safe*). Take a moment to be in awe and to share with the Lord the wonders you see! Give Him thanks for what He's made, and then give Him thanks for being in your life!

Just thinking.

Stop Trying to Peek

There are a couple of sayings that some parents use when dealing with nosy children: "Mind your business, grown folks are talkin'!" and "Stay out of grown folks' business!" (Those are the top two from my childhood.) In Job 37:5, Elihu tells us, "God does great things that are beyond our understanding." We pray and ask God to do things sometimes, and then instead of leaving it in His hands, we try to figure out exactly how and when He will do it. LOL. (I laugh because I do this.) In essence, we are trying to show God how to do things as we see fit! But we must remember Proverbs 14:12: "There is a way that seems right to a man, but its end is the way of death." God knows it all—period! He doesn't need us to suggest or show Him how to do His thing. Sometimes I would pray and after placing it in God's hands (or so I thought), I would sit and try to figure it out. Basically putting my hands all over the situation, and probably making it worse. God shares His glory with no man (Isa. 42:8), and He will wait until we decide to leave it alone before He does anything. Why? I guess so we don't think that what we did is what made things happen. Do we trust God? Do we believe He will provide all of our needs? Do we believe God knows what He is doing? If so, then why are we trying to get all in His business? Let go and let God!

JUST THINKING

Lastly, I recall my role in the kingdom of Christ was as a child of God. I realize now that I need to "stay out of grown folks' business"! LOL. How 'bout you?

Just thinking.

The Limp Limb

Okay. You are sitting in a meeting and the person talking has just said "um . . ." and "um, okay!" for the umpteenth time. LOL. And just before you are about to fall into a conscious coma, they announce a break. "Thank God!" you think to yourself. Then you push the chair back and try to get up. Surprise! Your leg is asleep. How many of you have had this happen? Oh, the agony, the tingling, the embarrassment of darn near falling out your chair (go ahead and laugh)! "What has a sleepy leg got to do with God?" you may ask. Well, walk with me. 1 Corinthians 12:12 tells us that we are one body, with many members. When all members are working well, the body is moving and functioning. However, when one member—just one—is sleeping, it can render the rest of the body immobile for a minute. Just like when your leg goes to sleep, when a member of the body of Christ sleeps, they slow the body down. I don't mean literally sleeping. I mean when we slack at our tasks or are not in tune with God's Word—that's sleeping. So, the arms, fingers, and toes are functioning fine, but it's that pesky leg again, slacking off on the job. So, the rest of the body must take time to awaken the member and get them back on track so we can move forward. We are all connected and have a role to perform in the body (1 Cor. 12:27). When one of us doses off, we all suffer. Are you the limpest limb? I'm trying not to be.

Just thinking.

Right Clothes, Wrong Cause

As I look around, I see more and more people starting and joining ministries. Personally, I think it's great; we need more soldiers. However, I have to stop at times and meditate on Matthew 7:15, "Beware of false prophets, which come to you in sheep's clothing, but inwardly they are ravening wolves." Take a second to ponder this as well. Paul, in Acts 20:28–30, warns leaders that they must keep watch and guard their flock. I am not knocking congregation growth, but tell me how one shepherd can keep watch over five thousand, or even twenty thousand, members? Paul declares, in Acts 20:26, that he is innocent of all men's blood because he told them the truth. Paul understood that it was not on his disciples if one man fell or was led astray—it was on *him*. He was the shepherd! There is a suggestion that having less than three thousand members means a shepherd is not moving in Christ. Just because we think a person is doing God's ministry does not mean their hearts and motives are right. So, what do we do? Well, Christ provided an easy way to tell the "real" from the "wolves"—check their fruits (Matt. 7:16–20). Are you being fed the Word

JUST THINKING

by a caring shepherd, or are you being fed empty words by a ravenous wolf? Examine their fruit, not their clothes!

Just thinking.

P.S. Check mine, too, for I am only a man!

Change Ain't Comin'

If a person had a check for a million dollars, never cashed it, and yet was always complaining of being broke, what would you think of them? I know I would be like, "shut up," or probably worse than that! LOL. But, sadly enough, I am that person. Sometimes I complain (usually to myself) about my situation, and yet I have not made a move to change it. I have every reason as to why it has not happened (Prov. 26:13). Yes, I have been lazy, and thus have an excuse. I think the scariest excuse I have is that I am waiting for God to change the situation. I may find myself waiting for a while! Just like the person with the check, I have all that I need to change my situation. You see, God planted it in me from day one. He has also provided the means for me to begin. I often make the mistake of waiting too much. I have noticed in my short time here on Earth that, often, God is waiting on me (to cash the check, so to speak). I can't pray that God will make me thinner, because He has already given me the strength to exercise. I can't ask for more money because He has provided me with the strength to earn a living and the wisdom to spend wisely. He won't knock the cigarette from my hand, but He has given me the will to resist temptation. I realized that change ain't comin'—I have to go to it, and my God is there to walk with me all the way! I have to at least get up and start walking toward it (John 5:8). Christ said, "the spirit is willing, but the body is weak" (Matt. 26:41). So true, so true. I know I am not the only one who has waited for change, right? (Okay, maybe I am, LOL.) But now I know I must boldly step out and show God that I am willing to try to change (James 2:20). Habits, finances, whatever! Change ain't comin'—we got to go to it! Got walkin' shoes?

Just thinking.

Shut Up

I have an issue. When I get excited about something or when I think I know something about a topic, I tend to talk a lot. I noticed Proverbs 20:12 says God made both "the hearing ear and the seeing eye." Where is the talking mouth? The *mouth*, I say! LOL. It is not present in this verse. I wonder why. Our mouths (and mine in particular) are not important here in this verse. God is stressing the importance of observation. We can miss a lot when we are talking. We can miss evidence of danger, signs of hope, or words of encouragement. We can miss all these things when we are busy talking. In this verse, God brings to light the importance of us just being quiet sometimes. "Watch and pray" (Matt. 26:41). It is good to communicate with others, and to share knowledge and wisdom. But let us be reminded that our words are reflections of our soul and our desires. We need to be protective of these things and mindful of what we say (Ps. 141:3). As I tell my son, and as I remind myself daily, it is impossible to talk and to listen at the same time. We may hear, but that doesn't mean we are listening. So, if we are always talking, how can we hear God?

    Just thinking.

Silence

Nowadays, it seems as if we all have to speak our minds. No matter the situation, we must make it known how we feel about it. Proverbs 29:11 says, "A fool vents all his feelings, but a wise man holds them back." Why? Why should I not speak my mind, not say how I feel? If an army were planning to attack a city, they would need to get inside of it in order to know the ins and outs of that city, correct? Well, we are a city, and our feelings, opinions, and emotions are the ins and outs of our city. Each time we speak, we give a little more of our blueprint and thus make it easier for our city to be attacked. When we speak, we reveal—whether we know it or not—what makes us tick, what makes us angry, happy, sad, and so forth. Why does the wise man hold back his feelings (or literally his "soul")? He is protecting his city from attack (Prov. 25:28). I usually speak out in an attempt to ensure that no one takes advantage of me, but how can that be, when God said He would fight all my battles? I had to ask myself, "Do I trust the Lord enough to say nothing?" How 'bout you?

Just thinking.

Skeletons in the Closet

Literally, what are skeletons? Bones, no flesh, no organs, and thus no life. I used to fear my skeletons. I feared that after coming to Christ, those that knew me before would bring up the past in an attempt to discredit or discourage me. I mean, we all have a past, but doesn't it always seem like *our* past is the worst? So, I did everything I could to distance myself from those skeletons, until recently. Let's look again: skeletons are bones with no flesh and thus no life! So, if there is no life to my former ways, then what is there to fear? My new ways are what dictate my living, not what I used to do. Ephesians 4:22–32 speaks on how we are to put off those past behaviors and God will show us mercy. I also look at it this way: If I was perfect from the beginning, then what need would I have of God's grace (Eph. 2:8)? We often fear the past because we do not know how it will be interpreted or viewed by *others*. Who cares about others! If God forgave us, what more do we need? The past is the past and does not become an issue in the present unless we make it one. Let the skeletons come out of the closet, share them as a testimony as to where God has brought you from. Besides, when the closet door is opened and those old bones fall out, they will shatter on the floor—freeing you completely!

Just thinking.

God's Child Too

It must have been hard on my parents. One child, the picture of goodness, and the other . . . Well, the other was "different." Yet, they did their best to love us both. I'm sure it was easier at times to love the "good" one, but nonetheless they loved us both. In the most basic sense, we were the equivalent of good and evil. Yet, there was love, not for the behaviors, but for the children themselves. In today's society, we are quick to blame, condemn, and ridicule "evil" people—the murderers, thieves, adulterers, etc. *We* condemn them. We pass judgement as to what they are worth to our society—yes, us Christians! Matthew 5:42–48 says we are to love our enemies, because there is no reward nor challenge in loving those that are nice and "pure." It's easy to forgive those who do little wrong, but it takes God's strength to forgive those that are always doing wrong. As I think back, God must have blessed my parents with all types of strength! LOL. But because of that love, here I am typing about God's Word. Yes, the wicked do some terrible things, but it is not our place to pass judgement or to retaliate (Rom. 12:19). Like it or not, God created the wicked, so doesn't that make them *His* children too? They may have lost their way, but isn't that why we are being used daily? Encounters with wicked people are not a chance for us to judge their actions, but a chance for God to judge *our* reactions.

Just thinking.

"I Ain't Got It!"

I was walking down the street one fall day when I ran into a homeless man. He commented on my "nice jacket" and jokingly asked if he could have it, with the understanding, in his mind, that I would not give it. As I began to remove my jacket, he stopped me. "Nah, man, that's okay, I was just joking!" But I urged him to take it. He refused and then asked, "You're a Christian, ain't you?" I was stunned and amazed! I had shared with him no scriptures nor confessed the Lord before him. He said he could tell by my actions. In Matthew 5:42, it says for us to give to whomever asks. Notice that it does not require us to make a judgement on whether they need it or not, but to give. In my life, I have also refused some that have asked, saying, "I ain't got it," when I really did. I just felt like they would waste it or spend it on drugs or liquor; I was wrong. Luke 6:38 says what we give we will receive, and we will be measured by the same measure that we measure others. (Okay, that was a bit tricky; breathe and read it again. Okay, ready? LOL.) God has blessed each of us with not just monetary possessions, but gifts as well. When we are asked to share, it is not an opportunity for us to pass judgement, but to be a living witness. Lastly, Proverbs 11:24 says, "There is one who scatters, yet increases." The more we give out, the more we receive. I know that in this crazy economic time, this seems furthest from our minds. But are we living for this crazy world or for our Heavenly Father? When you are asked to share, what is your response?

Just thinking.

Sista Souljah

Are we at war? Nah, not terrorism! Are *we* at war? I'll give you a second to think. . . . Okay, the answer is *yes*. That is why, in Ephesians 6:11, Paul urges us to, "Put on the whole armor of God." Armor is for battle, right? Daily, we are in a spiritual battle. We don't like to always dwell on it, but it is true. However, God did not send us out alone. He sent a "battle buddy" for us. In Proverbs 7:4, we are told to call wisdom our sister. She was created before anything else (Prov. 8:22–31). We can take solace in the fact that God has provided us with a partner in battle that will guide us, if we let her. Ponder this: God felt it vital to create her before anything else, and due to His great kindness, He offers her to us as a helper. Yes, we are in battle—daily. Be encouraged though, because unlike earthly wars, we already know the outcome of this one. Your sista is armed and ready to assist you! Report to duty, soldiers!

Just thinking.

Another Woman

The singer Usher titled one of his albums, "Confessions," on which he disclosed all the transgressions he'd committed, including cheating on his girl. Well, in this message, I will do the same. I must confess that even before marrying my wife, I was seeing another woman. Today, I must confess, I still communicate with her faithfully. She brings me prosperity, lengthens my life, gives me happiness, promotes me, and even provides me with a crown—all these things that my wife can't do. Why would I do, and even confess, such a thing? I share this with the hope of sharing my lady friend with others! Oh, yeah, I'll share! Why? God said it was okay. Yeah, the Word even encourages it. "Wisdom" is referred to as a woman in Proverbs 3:13–20 and 4:5–7. Why? Because only a woman could possess the type of beauty that wisdom holds. I know I could have shared this differently, but where is the fun in that? Please take some time and read up on my lady friend. We can all use her help. Trust me when I say your relationships will improve as a result of your "cheating"! LOL.

Just thinking.

What Gives Us the Right?

It had been about six months since I had last written a message, and basically a year since I had written any consistently. I had every reason in the book as to why: I just got married; I am working more hours; I need time for self, etc. Then I realized something—I had no right to stop! Reality check. If these writings are an inspiration to any and are based on God's Word, then I am not in control. Matthew 5:14 indicates that we are the light of the world. Yes, us! So, if we decide to cut our light off for whatever reason, there is the chance that someone may be living in darkness as a result. Yes, I know that God has many workers and a multitude of lights, but that still does not excuse us. What if, at the same moment, multiple lights decide to break for a while? These messages are more than just letters on a page, a morning pick-me-up, or a spiritual boost. For some, this is the closest they will get to God's Word. What is your light? Counseling, prayer without cease, caring for others, lending a helping hand, listening? Whatever it may be, please learn from my mistakes. When you shut that light off, even for a moment, you lose a connection with others and with God. I shut it off for a weekend and it turned into a year! Beware.

Just thinking.

Check It Out

Each day, we all go through the routine of checking our mail, our emails, and even our phone messages. Some even go so far as to "check" their spouses: Ladies, checking your male! LOL. (I don't care, that was funny!) We do this so that we can extract anything of value and discard things that are not of value. It is habit. Well, Christ requires the same in our spiritual walks. He asks that we "examine ourselves as to whether [we] are in the faith" (2 Cor. 13:5). Regarding our mail, we hold on to things like bills, checks, or any other potentially useful information. Relating to our spiritual walk, these things would be equivalent to keeping peace, kindness, integrity, and the like. We discard junk mail—"special offers," and other such things. The spiritual equivalent would be evil attitudes, lack of concern for others, or even lack of faith. Just as we check our mailboxes daily for needed and unwanted materials, the same can be done with the "mailboxes" of our souls. It takes about ten minutes (maybe longer for some—lots of junk, believe me, I know), but it is well worth it. Don't forget that in our case, mail is delivered on weekends too.

Just thinking.

Who You Be?

When the snow falls in winter and covers a house, does the house then become snow? Or when the rain falls and soaks a tree, does the tree suddenly become rain? Or lastly, when ice descends on an idle vehicle, does that vehicle then become ice? The answer is no! Many are reading these writings and saying to themselves, "This is common sense! He published *this*?" LOL. Wait, though. If the previously mentioned elements did not change the structures upon which they fell, then how come, when hard times fall on us, we often change? We change how we feel, how we think, and—most often—how we act. We view our situations as a part of who we are, or we let them define who we are! As if the elements of misfortune have the power to change "who we be"! I have recently found myself looking in the mirror and asking, "Who am I?" Simply because I noticed a change in my character—not a positive one, either. We are reminded in Romans 8:37 that "we are more than conquerors through him who loved us." This sounds good on Sundays and when all is well, but sometimes we forget it when the "snow," "rain," and "ice" fall on us. Be encouraged and keep looking up! Yes, the elements will fall and will immobilize us for a minute, but thank God for His son that dries them *all* up!

Just thinking.

"Phone Check, Punk!"

In many urban movies, there are jail scenes that involve a smaller inmate (who usually thinks he's "big time") being quickly coerced into giving up his precious phone time to another, much larger inmate. I know that the reality of such an event is serious, but I can't help but laugh when I hear the famous line, "Phone check, punk!" The purpose of the event is not so much that the larger inmate really needs the phone, it is more for him to demonstrate his authority over the other—let him know who's in control. Ironically, in my spiritual walk I have been "checked" many times! Not in the malicious way previously mentioned, but God regularly reminds me of who's in charge. Because of our free will, we sometimes lose sight of who is running things. Oh yeah, we tell others how God is "in control" of our lives, but we sometimes don't act like it. And just like a rebellious child, we have to be put back in our place. Sometimes it's subtle and sometimes it is as clear as day! LOL. Either way, after the "check," we are humbled and in awe of our own inabilities and God's power. Praise God! Nobody likes being reminded that they are not in control. I have come to believe that it is human nature to want control. But as we walk and talk more with Christ, we can easily see that it is in our best interest to turn over the reins. And I laugh at myself during these times because, just like the movie scene, I can just hear the Lord like, "This dude really thinks he's something!" A check is not a bad thing—it's a necessity. If you haven't experienced one, then you ought to be concerned (Job 5:17)!

Just thinking.

Money in the Bank

If you've ever watched a wealthy person, whether in person or on TV, you've noticed that they seem to walk and carry themselves with a certain confidence. I'm talking about the "my income *far* exceeds my bills" wealthy person. The wealthy person that has money in the bank to cover whatever may come or to do whatever they wish. They appear confident that no matter what happens, they got it covered. Amazing, isn't it? They have a swagger because they have what they need and more! The "new me" (we are all made new creatures in Christ) walks with a swagger. Oh, I walk with a swagger that some even take for arrogance—but it's not! It's a confidence in the fact that I have blessings in the bank! (Don't hold back, you know you want to smile! LOL.) Yes, you have them too! Christ told the disciples that *whatever* they asked in His name, His Father would provide (John 16:23). Money can come and go, can be spent, can be stolen or lost! But my blessings—oh, my blessings—will last as long as God does. Did you get that? The world gets its swagger from knowing and seeing. I get mine from knowing and believing. Get your swagger back and walk in your blessings. When they ask what's up with you, just tell 'em you got "blessings in the bank"!

Just thinking.

The Antidote

"For behold, I will send serpents among you, vipers which cannot be charmed, and they shall bite you" (Jer. 8:17). I watch *Animal Planet* sometimes and see the trainers working with the reptiles. If they get bitten by a venomous reptile, they must be rushed to the hospital for the antidote. If they receive it in time, they will only have the pain of the bite for a while, as well as the scar from the bite. If they do not receive it in time, more fatal complications may arise. We each encounter, daily, snakes and vipers that try to poison us with their bite. They are haters, control freaks, negatively-minded folks, and many other types. We are not always allowed to get away from them or to get rid of them, but when they bite, we have an antidote ready and waiting! Through our prayers, God can remove the poison from the wound they create and begin the healing process. But we must be aware of them. If we do not acknowledge being bitten, then the venom that was injected will begin to take effect. The beauty is that God is with us, always. Right after the bite, we can receive our dosage and move on. Daily, we are in the "snake pit," folks! Daily, we are face-to-face with vipers. Be on guard and be ready to receive your antidote when they begin biting—because they will bite! Some of us pride ourselves on being able to "charm"

them. If so, please refer back to line one. As the fishermen so excitedly say, "They are bitin' today!" Yeah, they are!
 Just thinking.

My Father's Forehead

I can say, with full conviction, that I have not been the best son to my parents. But through it all, they have remained faithful in supporting me and standing by my side (even though I used to think otherwise). I am particularly thankful for my father, and I wanted to share this message as a testimony to what God can do. In my younger days, I gave so much grief to my parents and caused much pain and suffering. For a period during my twenties, I was wondering why I was still living at home. I attributed it to my financial situation, lack of preparation, and other reasons. But I have now begun to understand one of the real reasons. Each morning before I left, I had the blessing of kissing my father's forehead and saying, "Love you, have a good day!" I am a witness to God restoring a relationship that I personally, consciously destroyed with my attitudes and actions. Although my father didn't always know how to respond, I know that he appreciated and loved the affection. As men, we are taught that our feelings for other men are only to be revealed in "manly" ways, and not through affection. But the mark of a true man is the security in himself to be able to display affection for those that he loves. My father is getting more mature (I would not dare to say older, LOL), and I want him to know that, although I acted a fool for a long time, I love and appreciate him now. I do not want to wait until he passes to say, "I shoulda, coulda, woulda." God alone is the restorer of relationships. He is the only one that can heal wounds of emotional pains. We each have played a part in destroying a relationship with someone we love, and God is directing us to healing. Let's be clear—I did not just wake up and say, "From now on I will kiss my parents each night." No! It was the Holy Spirit that guided me to display this affection. Our love is to be shown by action, not just words. What relationship have you helped to tear apart? Are you ready for God to mend it?

Just thinking.

Contempt

The idea that someone is below us, or is unworthy, is contemptuous. Fair enough. We are usually mindful enough to recognize this when dealing with people. I know that when talking with another person, I should not look down on them for any reason. A few years ago, though, I was shown that I was not as far along with this as I thought. When dealing with adults, it was easy to say, "We are all created equal, and I need to respect this person. They have something of value to offer as well." But when it came to children and teenagers, I often found myself speaking to them as if I were better than they were. Says who? Everyone God creates is expected to be loved and respected as His children (James 2:9). Who am I to judge? I remember times when I know God humbled me to speak to my students with the same respect that I would give another adult. Regardless of their age, they are people. If I choose to respect an adult more than I respect a child, then I alone have judged and shown partiality (Matt. 7:1). As I strive for the mark, I must recognize this partiality and ask God to help me change. I think of it like this: if God showed partiality to the old believers and loved and respected them more than the new believers, then we would be in an uproar. Imagine how the children feel!

Just thinking.

Treasure Chest

"Why do you teach? Why do you come to tutoring after teaching all day?" These are the questions that kids ask me daily. They can't figure out why, for little pay or for no pay, I am dedicated to working with youth. I, too, at one time, asked myself this question. At first, I recognized it as adhering to my calling, but then I was shown that it goes deeper than that. On Earth, when people want to store things of value, they may put them in a chest—a treasure chest. Money, jewels, gems, coins, and the like are considered valuable to man. So, we pursue and store up these things for our personal benefit. But Christ warns us that earthly treasures are open to theft, decay, and destruction. In the kingdom of God, they have no value! But the heavenly treasures are what Christ encourages us to store up. Integrity, compassion, humility, servitude, good character, and a heart of giving are just a few of the things that God values. "For where your treasure is, there your heart will be also" (Matt. 6:21). *Deep*. Go ahead, Jesus! LOL. Really, though, I often wondered how I found myself dedicated to helping others, and with no concern of the "worldly" priority of focusing on earthly treasures. I want to get to the throne, have God open my chest, see it radiate, and the Lord step back and say with a smile, "Well done!" Why do I serve the kids daily? Not because I am better than, but to make myself a better man! I ask then of you and me, where are our treasure chests? Heaven or Earth (Matt. 6:19–21)?

Just thinking.

And a Child Shall Lead Them

Have you ever watched a child? No, I mean *really* watched them? Carefree as can be, not a trouble in the world—unless, of course, a favorite toy gets broken! Seriously, though, even the world has to admit that children are the closest earthly form of God there is. Mainly because of the carefree attitude they display. They focus on nothing but enjoying themselves and are confident that their parents will provide. When they are hungry, they ask for food. When they are hurt, they are confident that their parents will provide care. When they are upset, they look to their parents to provide comfort. When they are tired, they rest in the comfort of knowing that their parents will provide a place of rest. Ultimate dependency—a child's way! So, how is my walk with my Father any different? Where is my carefree mentality of total dependency? The world says that life is too serious to just depend on a miracle God, and even some of us feel like if we don't stress over it, then it won't get done! I beg to differ. I have been that stressed out and worrisome soul that "must get things done," and it drained me! I had to ask myself, "What kind of testimony am I giving?" Honestly, if all the Christians you knew before you were saved, were worrisome and stressed folks, would you have been eager to turn to the Lord? Our faith stands on the foundation that God is the *Father*—period! It's not laziness, not by any means. But I do believe that we can lean on God's divine favor and provisions more and, as a result, stress less. A child is given tasks and then allowed to play. As parents and adults, we understand that they must have this balance—after all, they are children, right? I checked my Word and found that I, too, am a child—God's child (Gal. 3:26), that and Christ died so that I can be free (Gal. 5:1)! Carefree! Worry free! Stress free! And any other free you can imagine. The chains of control, stress, anxiety, anxiousness, doubt, and financial burdens have been broken for those that have faith in the Father! Believe it, receive it, and walk boldly in your freedom! Say it with me: "Give us, free us!" And God says, "I have!" (John 3:16).

Just thinking.

Disciples Do Panic

It would be nice to believe that the faith of followers of Christ is never shaken. It would be nice to see ourselves as strong enough in the Word to never have a situation cause us to question ourselves or our faith in the Lord. However, I will be the first to admit to being human, and this very thing happens to me. There are times when I slip and fall—sometimes hard! But the Lord knows us and our hearts. I recall the account of the disciples and Christ crossing the ocean in a boat when a storm arose (Matt. 8:24). Now, let's be clear—these twelve men had seen, touched, heard, watched, and been with Christ in the flesh for a time, and it can be said that they had a knowledge of His greatness and power. But in the midst of the storm, they all began to panic! These very men who knew our Saviour in the flesh and had seen Him heal the blind, lame, and sick, began to panic! But their reaction to their panic is the real lesson. Who did they cry out to? "Teacher, don't you care that we're about to drown?" (Mark 4:38). They cried out to Christ. He could have said something like, "Here I am trying to sleep, and these jokers are crying about the rain. They know I am Jesus! Aight, rain stop, wind stop. Can I sleep now? I got folks to heal in the morning!" But the Lord used their moment of fear of death to increase their fear and respect for Him (Matt. 8:27). God sees and knows all, even when we cannot fully understand the situation. I encourage you, as I encourage myself, to be mindful of shaky faith and disbelief. It happens to all of us—just ask the twelve disciples. But when it does happen, cry out to the Lord and let Him encourage your heart, spirit, and mind! If men who walked with Christ were open to a moment of shaky faith, then I know I will have an episode or two—or three, or four, or . . . You get the point!

Just thinking.

Listen, Listen

Christ says that His sheep know His voice and follow Him because they know it (John 10:4,27)! I had to ask myself, "Do I know His voice?" Sometimes I can get so caught up in praising, worshiping, and prayer requests that I forget to listen. If Abraham hadn't listened, his son would have been killed. If Solomon had not listened, no words of wisdom would have flowed to create the book of Proverbs! I must say, it is easy to get consumed in self and forget to listen to the Father. But any healthy relationship requires that both sides listen to each other—not just hear, but listen (1 John 5:14–15). And as I recall, we have a personal relationship with Christ. John 8:47 says, "He who belongs to God hears what God says. The reason you do not hear is that you do not belong to God." That's deep! Think about it like this: If your mom calls, you know as soon as she says "hello" who she is. If your lover calls, you know who it is by the "Hey, baby!" But if God calls, would you know for sure that it is Him on the line? Tuning into God's voice is vital—as we are in trying times—and it is key to our walk with Christ. The old folks say that God blessed us with two ears and one mouth so we could listen twice as much as we speak!

    Just thinking.

Nothing to Give

As I set my mind to pray for words, I realized that I had nothing to say! I had no divine inspiration, no eloquent word play, cunning diction, or persuading dialogue that would spark the inner spirit of the reader. I had nothing! And then, it hit me—it was never *me* in the first place! The ability to analyze truth, place into word form what my spirit contemplates, or even spread the gospel of Christ is explicitly based on the strength of Christ Himself. Honestly, I have sat down to many write times before, without prayer or seeking God's guidance first, wishing to express a thought that would inspire anyone who read, only to be blocked, stumped, stupefied, and rejected. How can I portray ownership of ideas that were given, not created? Imagine, for a moment, Matthew proclaiming, "Yeah, that bit in the Bible about Christ? Yeah, I wrote that one! Good, ain't it?" Or Paul saying, "Man, I spent hours thinking of what to say to those churches; it was hard, but I did it!" Or even the great Solomon uttering, "Between counting my riches and keeping track of my women, writing was a struggle, but I did it!" God is the provider of what we have to offer. Before we were created, He placed in us all the things that He planned later to bring out of us (Phil. 2:13)—the gifts, talents, thoughts, ideas, etc. (Rom. 12:4–6). Without Him, we have nothing to give, believe it or not. God is the key to unlocking what we possess, whether we acknowledge Him or not. He makes it happen. All good things come from Him (James 1:17). All this is to say, when you feel you have nothing left to give, remember who was supplying it in the first place. Once you remember that, then it is easy to see that *His* supply never ends (1 Cor. 2:9; Ps. 147:5), and we have direct access to His supply. Instruments, tools, vessels—none of which work under their own power but must be guided and handled by the craftsman (Rom. 9:21–25). When I have nothing to give, I pray that God will give His all.

Just thinking.

Our Right to Complain

It's amazing that the small book of Jonah contains so much wisdom. I am not much of a complainer, but I do so at times. But the book of Jonah has shown that I have no right! When Jonah was in the desert heat, God created for him a plant—or "gourd" for the philosophers (Jon. 4:6–10)—that provided Jonah with shade. Now, with the intense heat, Jonah was happy about the shade provided for him. But then God created a worm to destroy the plant, and sent an even stronger heat, and Jonah complained due to his suffering. (I must say, I would have been a bit troubled as well, to put it lightly. LOL.) But God asked Jonah if he had a right to be mad about something that he neither labored to plant or grow. This was when I began to realize something. If all good things come from God, who is sovereign—which means He does what He pleases— then doesn't He reserve the right to take what He pleases as well (Ps. 115:3)? I often look at my life and am thankful for what I have, but rarely do I consider what my position would be if He removed it all! In reviewing this passage, it is plain for me to see that if God chose to remove the blessings that He bestowed, I have no right to complain. It sounds straightforward and harsh, but it's true. We trust that God is our Father and provider, and we really don't fathom what our mindset or "heartset" would be if He stopped providing or allowed a time of drought. I have experienced drought in different forms, and I can recall that during those times I had some praises, as well as some problems with how things were going. But by God's mercy, I was forgiven and brought through. When the tree, the shade, the provisions, and the blessings no longer fall from the throne, will we praise continually or complain constantly? Jonah serves as a great example!

Just thinking.

You Don't Belong Here

In our hearts was placed a calling, a purpose, and a desire to complete certain tasks. Some of us have wholeheartedly embraced these callings, and others have not! In my short time on this earth, I have tried to do many things, including run a business, property investments, and even a desk job. But truth be told, I never really felt comfortable in any of them. Additionally, those that I worked with probably sensed that I was not cut out for these things either. They knew that I did not belong there! Even my current position as a teacher is not the final destination. I look at Jonah and see a man that felt that what he was "called" to do was so out of range from what he was comfortable doing that, instead of trying, he ran (Jon. 1:3). He sought refuge with sailors. Now here is the deep part: during this retreat, Jonah's actions caused others to suffer for as long as he was with them (Jon. 1:4–5). Did you get that? When we do not adhere to our true calling when called, we cause others to suffer with us. Not only did the men on the boat suffer from the storm, but the people in the city of Nineveh continued to suffer under their evil ways (Jon. 3:1–4). Generally, when we think about our callings, we focus on what effect it will have on us and those in our immediate circle, but we forget that our God sees beyond us!

All is not lost, though. As soon as Jonah left the ship, look how God was glorified. He took that moment of suffering and used it to save souls (Jon. 3:10). The point being, the sooner we embrace our gifts and talents and allow God to use us, the sooner those that God will bless by using us can benefit and those that are burdened by our presence can be freed. I know that one of my callings is to be a writer, but I turned away for so long that I thought it was just a fantasy. But in His time, God increased the conviction in my heart to the point that I had to share. It is a blessing to write these words and share them with others. The job that drives you crazy, the position that has you frustrated, the people that make you bonkers are all yelling the same thing: "You don't belong here!" Will you listen now or take them down with you? There's a whale waiting!

Just thinking!

Can You See What I See?

I used to think I was crazy. I would see a bright spot in every situation, or I would see the outcome of a seemingly negative problem in a positive way. Really, I thought I was *loco*! I thought this because no one else saw these things the way I did—in a positive light. Or they would ask using that I-hear-you-but-I-don't-think-it-will-work-that-way voice, "Well, what are you going to do?" Surprisingly, just as my heart let me believe, God responded to my faith with positive outcomes (Mark 11:24). Don't get me wrong, not everything turned out the way I wanted, but it did turn out positively. All this is to say, we have a choice. We can either focus on what we see or have faith and focus on what we believe. In 2 Corinthians, Paul reminds us of this by saying, "While we do not look at the things which are seen, but at the things which are not seen" (2 Cor. 18). I love this verse! Faith is eternal and faith is how we came to know Christ in the first place. Believing that all things will work to our good is vital, because as Paul also reminds us, "We are hard-pressed on every side, yet not crushed" (2 Cor. 8). Each man is given different gifts from God (1 Cor. 12). (As you can tell, I have been in those letters.) But the gift of faith is one that we all need. For without it, our belief means little. The title of the thought "Can you see what I see?" means simply this: When all those around us say it will never happen, can you look beyond and see that God's Word says it will? Be encouraged, be encouraged, be encouraged!

Just thinking.

The Role of the Wife

In today's society, the role of the wife has taken a drastic turn. For whatever the reason—be it financial, emotional, or the like—the role of the wife has gone from caretaker to co-provider (sometimes even primary provider). They have taken on the responsibilities of their male counterparts without flinching! (Go ahead, ladies!) Although some can balance both the laborious tasks of work and home with assistance from their husbands, many find it challenging and tiresome. And when the energy of that hardworking wife (and they work so hard) has been spent having to help provide, doesn't that drain them of some of that needed energy to bless their homes? Now, before the independent women begin to get up in arms, hear me out! Christ is the "bridegroom" of the church. Which in turn makes the church His wife! (Some of y'all already see what's coming—a "good job" sticker for ya! LOL.) In some cases, the church has taken on the model of the modern-day wife, becoming more and more focused on providing and accepting some of the responsibilities of the husband (Christ) in order to help out. For example, many of our churches are focused on financially providing for themselves through things such as the selling of sermons, books, videos, and the like. If I recall, the Bible said that God would supply all of our needs. Now, the trick to this is that the wife (the church) is bringing in something to the relationship with its groom (Christ), and so it is easily justified as to why the church would accept this responsibility. The more money that can be generated, the bigger the buildings, thus more people can come in, and thus more souls saved, right? Right? Did Christ ask us to take on these burdens? The reference to the wife earlier was based on what is happening in our worldly society. The Word encourages us to be in the world and not of it. See, when the wife (the church) is focusing on being the breadwinner, that energy then has to be spread out in order to be the breadwinner, provider, supporter, mother, and caretaker. In the same light, that church that now focuses on "increasing the kingdom" (being a breadwinner) has taken its focus away from personal relationships with its members, being a sustained light to those in darkness and even giving selflessly. "One man plants, one man waters, and God will bring the increase" (1 Cor. 3:7). *God will bring the increase.* Has taking on these tasks distracted us from our responsibilities? Each of us is the church, God's temple. I have to ask myself daily, "Am I holding fast to the Word, or am I changing with the world?" God created this world long before we existed, and I don't recall Him needing our help then. What makes us think He needs our help now? This message was for me, but I hope that another is blessed by it! I learned that to be a good bride, I need to stay in my lane and out of God's way. Just sit back and let Him be the man!

Just thinking.

P.S. Don't take my word for it, either. Check out the scriptures for yourself: Isaiah 62:5, Matthew 9:15, 7:15–23, and Ephesians 5:23.

Silence on the Set

I pray that all are well. God is faithful in keeping His children, so I hope this reaches each of you in good health. I learned this month the meaning of the scripture "there is a time to speak, and a time to remain silent" (Eccles. 3:7). God had me be silent these past few weeks. I was eager to begin the new year with amazing insights and inspiration. However, a bridle was put over my mouth, and I was encouraged to listen. Sometimes, we are so eager to tell someone about something that we don't take the time to listen. Taking the time to listen can be the difference between life and death (Deut. 30:19). I am a talker at times (yeah, I can run off at the mouth), but it was humbling and enlightening to just listen to what God had to share and to what He was saying through others. I am thankful to be writing again. I look forward to daily insight from the Lord, and fresh words for everyone—including me! Be encouraged at all times, and what weighs heavy on your heart, take it to your Brother and leave it there. Listen closely and you will hear what is being said!

Just thinking.

The Message, Not the Messenger

I'll get straight to it. When Christ came, His appearance was totally different from that of any of the others claiming to know the Lord and His ways (Isa. 53:1–12). He was not draped in fine linen and tassels and all the getup that the pharisees wore back then. He appeared to be just a regular person. The point being, when it comes to God and His Word and messages, we cannot get caught up in who is giving it; let's not forget He used a donkey to speak His word (Num. 22:21–39)! We often get caught up in who is bringing forth the Word and who they are, but let God deal with that! Listen close and test the words by the Word (1 Thess. 5:20–21)! I say this because I know I have missed plenty of messages from the Lord simply because of who He used to send them. Do I hear His voice and receive the message? Or do I worry about the messenger? If we know God's Word and His voice, we don't have to be concerned with who He uses to get our attention.

Just thinking.

Attitude Adjustment

We get what we give (Gal. 6:7). I had the privilege of discussing some anger management issues with some youth recently. What they said was amazing. One child said that when two people are arguing, and one is yelling and the other is speaking calmly, then the one that is yelling looks really stupid. Also, they said that when both persons are yelling, they both look stupid and nothing is accomplished! This says a lot. When we get so upset that we must yell and scream, we have lost control (Prov. 25:28). When we have lost control, we no longer have the ability to understand, to reason, or to hear God's voice (1 Pet. 5:6–8). Usually in the midst of this loss of control we say things and do things that we later regret, no matter how much we think our anger is justified (Prov. 21:23). Think of it this way: When Christ came face-to-face with critics and haters, do you think He spent His time yelling and screaming to get His point across? I think not! (Okay, there was that one time in temple (Matth. 21:12), but I still think he was cool, calm, and collected. I see him just sliding through the temple like a "G.") I believe He knew that the moment He countered His critics with the same hate and anger they were giving Him, He would have fallen into their trap! How could He preach peace and love, but in the same breath yell and argue with His brothers? I imagine Christ calm, cool, and collected, telling His adversaries, "I am here to show a new way!" and walking off. Now that's "gansta." LOL! We are not perfect, and we will fall short at times, but if we are to represent our God, we must reflect Him in all situations (2 Cor. 5:20). Anger is contagious, and the enemy seeks to infect us daily. Let us all be mindful of how we respond to anger, for it is a trap for our souls! Love is the only counterattack for hate!

Just thinking.

Still Going

In the midst of our walk with Christ we are allowed to go through tough times—both mentally and physically. I have to say, for me, the mental is the harder of the two to endure. Focusing my thoughts on Christ in the midst of everything is hard sometimes. I cannot always put my finger on the cause of my mental anguish, and so it is hard to ask God to remove it. I know the Holy Spirit can intercede and ask on my behalf, but it is hard. However, in the midst of this, I know that God is still with me, and honestly, this is enough for me to keep going. God knows when we need to be encouraged. He sends a message or even an angel to encourage us in the midst of strain. I pray that you will be blessed by this message and recognize when your spirit is missing that joy that keeps you going. When you feel it, immediately ask for God's presence and peace. This may not remove the situation or thought, but it will allow God to move in the situation, which is all that He asks of us. Trust that He is in control of *all* things! We are human and we will get down sometimes, but we can be encouraged in the Christ we serve, can count all our joys and keep going (1 Cor. 9:24). Be encouraged that whatever it is we face, God will bring us through. Just remember those

are not our footprints in the sand. Keep going soldiers, our General has guaranteed the victory!
　　Just thinking.

Chain Reaction

I used to do some crazy things to people. I mean, downright *mean* things—especially when it came to women! At the time, I did not care about anyone but me. But when the Lord came into my life, it was not as easy. When God came into my life, He showed me not only the sin I was committing, but also how it affected others, and this caused me pain (Isa. 57:20–21). The conviction of the Holy Spirit is real. It is directly connected with my sin and the Lord knows this (Rom. 8:10). He gave us this helper so that we would not be oblivious to the sin we commit. But here is where it gets rough. Not only does sin come with the cost of conviction, but it also opens the door to the enemy (the accuser) to condemn and bring guilt. When we become aware of our sin and ask God for forgiveness, it is cast away. However, the enemy will try to bring it back, like a dog does a tossed stick. God knows this, and He knows that it is difficult for us to ignore the accusations that Satan makes of us: "You were wrong, and you were supposed to be a Christian!" and "You keep doing the same dumb thing—you ain't never going to get it right." God loves us and wants us to be the best we can. He knows the sins we will commit before we do them. He knows the accusations Satan will try to make as a result of the sin, and so God offers us guidance and advice to avoid sin—His word and voice. He knows that when we do not avoid sin, we are open to the attacks of the enemy. The results of sin are not just blemishes on our armor of righteousness, they are holes through which Satan tries to puncture us with guilt and ridicule. The results of sin are a chain reaction or domino effect, and lust was my first domino to start mine. I have caused many a reaction in my time—as short a time as it has been—and I have been poked by Satan's daggers. I offer this as food for thought so that another can prevent a hole in their armor. There is often debate about what sin is; when you are convicted by the Holy Spirit, you will surely know! Ask and it will be answered.

Just thinking.

Anonymous Angels

Have you ever encountered a person you did not know that was a blessing to you? It was as if they were the answer to a prayer, but you did not know them. I have had this experience many times. It is wild! It was as if God sent an angel to answer my prayers. But as I get to know the Lord more, I see the roles switching. More and more, I run into people that I have never met before and find that God uses me to advise, provide, assist, and encourage them. When all is said and done, I realized that there was no exchange of names or titles! I thought at first that I was being rude, but I am learning that there is no need for a name exchange. When the moment has passed, and the person looks back on the blessing, they cannot say, "Oh yeah, so-and-so was the one who did that for me." Nope. They can recall no name, and therefore God receives all His glory. We are servants, and servants are not called to be recognized. If you can recall movies in which servants are present, it is almost always their duty to remain inconspicuous. They just serve and get out of the way. The funny part about it is, even in the movies, the masters get the credit for having such good servants. Later on, the servant may be rewarded by their masters for getting them recognition, but if not, the servant still performs well. What master do you know that deserves more credit than God? In order for Him to get it though, we have to serve and get out of the way! Remain anonymous (2 Thess. 1:11–12).

Just thinking.

His Eyes Are on You, Not Them

As a teacher, I encounter the challenge of imparting knowledge and guidance to the youth. However, many times this information is brushed off or not fully digested. I used to struggle with the fact that my kids did not see the benefits of what I was giving. After a conversation with a friend this morning, God addressed this situation from a spiritual standpoint. God is watching us, and we are held accountable for what *we* do, not what others do. We can only share and encourage, but it is up to those that we share with to make the decisions that will benefit them. If they choose not to take heed, it is on them. However, it is difficult sometimes, when we have a heart for helping, to watch another person make decisions and take actions that will ultimately hinder them. But we must remember God is in control. I look at it this way: If I had not made the mistakes that I did, and fell when I fell, I would not know the Lord the way I do. Sometimes God allows us to suffer for our actions in order to strengthen us and give us a better perspective on who He is. As advisors, teachers, friends, and people, we must remember that God is not concerned with what others are doing. He is watching what we do. While being ignored and watching people do their own thing, do we still have the heart to share with them? I remember when I would not receive what God was telling me, but He never stopped talking to me. We can't control what others do, and God is not concerned with what they do. He wants to see what we will do in the midst of it all. Remember this: When we go home and meet our Savior, He will not ask, "What did they do?" He will ask, "What did *you* do?"

Just thinking.

Righteous or Perfection

There are plenty of accounts of righteous men and women in the Bible—Job, Daniel, Noah, Abraham, Ruth, etc. However, of the many stories in the Bible, I can only recall one person ever being referred to as perfect, and that is Christ—without flaw! But the others that were righteous were used in mighty ways. Some of them had issues, and some were reformed heathens! (I can relate! LOL.) But none of them were perfect. Righteousness is not perfection. Being righteous is a posture and attitude that begins with our relationship with Christ, and then grows out of our hearts and into our actions. I was once confused with the idea of "the path of righteousness." I had led myself to believe that it meant never making mistakes or failing at serving the Lord. Yeah, right! I can recall times during which I believed that my righteousness was infallible! Picture that! And because of this posture, when I fell, I fell hard, and it was hard to forgive myself for my faults. God has only asked us to pursue righteousness, and even when we attain this, "it is as filthy rags" (Isa. 64:6) in comparison to His. We are not perfect, and will never be, until we head home to glory. Be easy and walk straight. Righteousness is our goal, but even if we never reach it, we are on the right path!

Just thinking.

BE STILL

Here's proof that God is in control! Although I was physically worn out, I was prepared and ready to complete the task of staying after work to help my kids more, and then head to tutoring at another location. However, as the afternoon announcements blared through the speakers, I was told that due to the threat of a tornado, all students were to ride the bus and there would be no after-school activities. Then I headed to the parking lot to give a coworker a jump in the pouring rain! (I know I saw at least three cats and two dogs, LOL!) I ran through a puddle of water and it caused my engine to flood, cutting my car off. We had to find another person to give her the jump. They left, and I sat and waited for my engine to dry, during which time I prayed. We had canceled the other tutoring due to the weather as well, so I had nowhere to be. Thankfully so, because my car was not going anywhere anytime soon. The point being, God knows when we need a break. He knows when we just need to be still. He also recognizes that we are a stubborn bunch, and unless He makes it plain and clear that we need to be still, we will keep on going! My car not starting could have been a burden or a blessing, depending on my perception. I thank God that He allowed me to see what He was doing, and to not be concerned about getting somewhere, when He had already planned my break! Keep pushing, keep going, and keep working for the Lord. Be ready to do so, even when you think you are ready to give up. God will provide the rest when you really need it!

Just thinking.

Free Time

I know that many of us don't even know what free time is. With all that must be done during the course of a day, it seems as if there isn't enough time. But what I mean by this is a little different. When I say free time, I mean giving your time freely. We are told that we reap what we sow (Gal. 6:7). If we give our money faithfully, we will reap the benefits of sharing. Well, what about giving our time? That is a sacrifice I was unfamiliar with until recently. I thought the only way to serve or to sacrifice was to give financially to God's work. Boy, was I wrong (LOL)! Time is a rare commodity, even more so than money nowadays. It is hard enough to find the time to take care of things in the course of a day, let alone to find extra time to give away. I am not talking about the committees and boards we sit on at church either. I am talking about taking time to share with someone who really needs an ear to listen, or a friend to share the afternoon with. I am aware of the day-to-day responsibilities we are faced with, but I also recall that "only what we do for God will last" (1 Cor. 15:58). Each day, God takes time to listen to all of our problems, complaints, concerns, and cares, and so I realized that it is only right for me to extend that same privilege to others. How can we lead someone to Christ if we never take the time to hear them calling out to Him? Believe me, if we each took two hours a week to spend with a person for no other reason than to share our blessings with them, our lives would be that much more fulfilling. Not to mention that it would make our Father smile. "Look at my child, trying to be like Daddy!" He would say with pride. (LOL.)

Just thinking.

More Than Enough

Lately, I have been running without stopping. I find myself really fatigued when it is time for my next move. During this time, I have found that my need for God's strength and endurance is more prevalent than ever. When I get tired, I am impatient, irritable, unfriendly, and even rude! I just don't want to be bothered. Try telling a room full of kids that you are too tired to help them. Good luck! Thank the Lord for having more than enough. Before each task, I find that I must pray for God's patience, love, understanding, and strength (Isa. 40:29). When I do, and begin walking in what I asked for, I find that time is irrelevant and passes with ease (2 Thess. 3:16). I find that my disposition is more kind and more caring. I realize that by letting it be known that I need His presence to carry me, He does just that—He carries me through. But when I finish what needed to be done, I also find that I have more energy left! He will never put more on us than we can bear with His help (1 Cor. 10:13)! God knows that what He asks us to do is too much for us to do on our own (Isa. 26:12). If this were not true, then the credit would possibly go to us (Isa. 42:8). God gives us a task and the insight to recognize that we need His help to complete it. When we do humble ourselves and ask for help, He gives more than enough, believe me! Can't find the strength to finish the day? Need more strength to share quality time with your family after a long day of work? Need the extra patience to do homework with the kids at night? Try Christ! He's more than enough!

Just thinking.

Be Encouraged

If we were to look around, we would see someone that is in a worse position than we are. We must be encouraged by the fact that we are loved by our Father, and that He has not allowed things to get worse than they are. We are only given what we can bear! Take one minute to focus on nothing but the positive things happening in your life—honestly, do it. Stop focusing on the negative things for one minute. I find that when I do this, I end up spending more than a minute. It is worth a try. Let God remind you of what He is doing in your life.

Just thinking.

Be Ready to Pray

There is a lot going on in the world these days, and if we focus too much on those things, they can be very overwhelming. It is good to know that we have a refuge in these crazy times (Ps. 46); however, some do not. For whatever reason, some do not know that there is one who can give them peace in the midst of all this chaos. Furthermore, there are some who know the one, but for whatever reason cannot bring themselves to talk to Him. As a follower of Christ, it is my responsibility to be ready and willing when God places me in front of anyone who needs to talk with Him but may be unwilling or hesitant. It is a fact that they must humble themselves, but sometimes God allows us to intercede for them (1 Tim. 2:1). I have found that if I am not prepared to pray on the behalf of others, then I myself am in a sad state. If a person was poor and needed money, and I knew of a generous millionaire that would gladly help them out, I would speak to the millionaire on their behalf and ask him to help them. It is the same in our spiritual walk. Daily we encounter the spiritually poor, and our Father is a generous millionaire waiting for them, or for us, to ask for help. Daniel spent nights praying on behalf of his city and asking God to show mercy (Dan. 9:19–23). He didn't have to—he chose to, he was ready to. When we are face-to-face with the spiritually poor, what will be our response? "Figure it out" or "Let me introduce you to my wealthy friend"?

Just thinking.

Can't Find Time? Make it

My daily routine consists of event after event. From working, to writing, to tutoring, to fathering, to getting ready for the next day—not to mention the unexpected happenings. I found that I had no time to breath on certain days, or that I was so tired that I just fell out! I did not have time to study and read the Word. I understood that it was essential to my walk, but I just didn't have time! And then it hit me (kind of like how a parent pops a child upside the head when they don't find time to clean that room of theirs or to wash those dishes)! If I can't find time to study and read, I have to make time. Yes, my daily schedule is hectic, but if someone told me that they wanted to meet me to give me a million dollars, I *would* make the time for that! What reading and studying the Word offers is worth far more than that million (2 Cor. 5:1–4). So, I have to create moments in which to sit and be at peace with God's Word. Life is full of choices, and God simply tries to guide us in the direction of the best choice. But if we don't have time to listen to His directions, His word, then how can He guide us? Life is hectic, but God's Word has the power to put it all in perspective, if we make time to see and hear it! A wise man can learn from the mistakes of others. Here's a chance to learn from mine!

Just thinking.

Temporary Residency

It is without doubt that pride, jealousy, envy, arrogance, and even fear will rear their ugly heads in our lives. I am not talking about them coming from other folks, either! As humans, these are the very vices that the enemy can easily use to tear us down. The trick is that the enemy uses our own rationale to justify them (Acts 5:3), and in some cases he will even back them with the "Word" (I keep forgetting that he knew it long before I did!). I recently had a battle with fear. It overtook me for a minute, and I found myself back to my old ways of hiding out in the "dungeon" until I felt better. I did not consistently pray, I simply talked to God on an as-needed basis. I felt so empty and incomplete during this time that I did not even enjoy the things that normally would lift my spirits. I tried poetry, I tried zoning out with a movie—I tried! Each event only pushed me further into anger and fearfulness. I feared what I would become if I became what God wanted me to become. Crazy, ain't it? I feared that if I became the success that He said I will be, then I would not remain humble. Then a special friend mentioned the fact that I could be hiding behind God's Word in an attempt to hide my fears (2 Cor. 11:3). Remember, the enemy knows the Word! "Wait!" the enemy said to me. "God doesn't want you to make these moves yet. What if you fail?" Sadly enough, I didn't listen closely enough to hear that it was the wrong voice. Fear, arrogance, and any other vice the enemy may use are only powerful when we allow them to get into our spirits. Be encouraged that, yes, these things will come upon us, but we determine how long they stay with us. Fear is of the enemy. God said He would do great things through me. How? I do not know, but I hold on to *His* Word! Listen closely and be sure that the residents of your spirit are truly supposed to reside there! If not, serve them their notice of eviction!

Just thinking.

Praise, No Matter What

It is easy to give God praise when everything is going your way, but what about when it isn't? I don't mean major troubles and hardships, just the day-to-day disappointments. Like when your plans get flipped around and what you thought was going to happen does not. Does God still get the praise for being in control? I have, in the past, been a victim of my own withholding of praise. The funny part about it is that it was not God who punished me for not giving Him his due praise, it was me! When I did not acknowledge God and praise Him for just being Him, and being in control, I was not happy at all. There was—is—a need inside of me to give praise where praise is due. Not because of what He has done, but because of who He is. When I did not do this, I felt incomplete for not giving Him praise. So as a result, I try to give God praise in the midst of it all. When things don't go according to what I thought would happen, or even if they do, I try to give God His props. When you know Christ and have a relationship with Him, there is no way to go by and not stop and acknowledge His presence and authority daily. Our spirits crave this. Truly and ultimately, that is what we are built for! I have denied Christ His proper due more times

than the disciples on the morning of the Crucifixion—but no more! Give props where props are due!
    Just thinking.

Repeat Offenders

Imagine being trapped in a life you did not ask for. Bound by another and forced to serve out of fear of punishment! Your every waking moment is destined for the pleasing of another. Then after long suffering, fervent prayer, and submission, God allows for you to be freed from the situation. Once free, you instantly thank Him, and serve Him out of obligation. But after a while it wears off, and you begin to do your own thing. Then, God allows you to fall back into bondage, and when you cry out, He saves you again. Once free, you instantly thank Him and serve Him, but after a while, you start doing your own thing again. Should God punish you for your disobedience? Would you punish you if you were God? Well, this is the story of the children of Israel—the repeat offenders. They, better than anyone at the time, knew God's power, and yet they continually turned away from Him. But for some strange reason (I think they call it love), God continually saved them from themselves and brought them back into the fold (Jer. 3:22). Some of us are repeat offenders; I humbly admit to it. We find ourselves blessed by God in a way we could never imagine, and for a moment He is all we know. But sure enough, that "spiritual high" wears off and we are back at it again! Do not be discouraged, there is mercy for us (Jer. 3:12; Acts 3:19).

JUST THINKING

By no means am I condoning backsliding, but we must know that it can happen. When it does, do we sit in it and allow ourselves to be judged by self or by others? Or do we return to our Savior and move on? See, it took the whole book of Judges and then some for the children of Israel to understand. How long will our own chapter of backsliding last?

Just thinking.

Angels of Light?

During one of my tutoring sessions, God allowed me to read and interpret 2 Corinthians 11:13–15. One student was asked to read and interpret this verse for Bible class. I have to say it was a blessing for me. In these crazy days and times, it is easy to be led astray. This verse focuses on false apostles (or prophets, ministers, and the like). It is easy to portray one's self as a part of the body of Christ to those that do not know Him. But you know what? It may be even easier to do so with those that do know him. Some lean to their own knowledge and wisdom when it comes to discerning the things of God—which I found to be a grave error (Prov. 3:5–6). When we come to know God on a personal level, we get comfortable with hearing His voice—knowing some of His ways and the like. But remember, Satan himself was once an angel of light (2 Cor. 11:14), and he knows God's Word and ways better than any of us! If Satan himself portrays himself as a light to the world, then it is no wonder why we have so many false apostles doing the same (2 Cor. 11:15). Only God knows who is who, and it is only through Him that we can protect ourselves from being led astray. We have to keep in mind that since the beginning, man has been led astray. (Does anyone remember that guy named Adam? LOL). If Adam—a man who knew God intimately—can be led astray, then, without God guiding us, we are in for it! All this is to say, before we follow any leader, we need to make sure they are following Christ (1 Tim. 4)! Ask and God will show us (1 John 4).

Just thinking.

Little Steps

When it comes to major things, I have no problem recognizing my need for God's help. You know—bills, finances, conflicts with people, etc. These things present themselves to me with an obvious need for help. However, I have come to see in recent days that the little things require His help too. What do I mean by "the little things"? How about waking up with no alarm clock, making it to work early or on time, speaking to my coworkers with a pleasant tone, or even smiling? They all seem like tiny activities that should not require bothering the Lord, but they are so much easier to do when I do ask for help (Prov. 3:5–6). By asking for help, I am exercising my faith in what the Lord can do. By putting these "small tasks" in the Lord's hands, it makes it that much easier for me to put the big things in His hands and leave them there. Think of it this way: When a child is learning to walk, they take small steps. These small steps give them not only the confidence to walk farther, but they also strengthen their leg muscles in order to sustain themselves over those longer distances. If we only trust God with the big things, eventually our "faith muscles" will give out—unless we strengthen them with smaller tasks. God can move in any situation. In fact, He asks us to trust Him with all of our burdens—big or small. I can't tell you how amazing it is to see God move in what I think are small situations. It is mind blowing. Try it! What have you got to lose?

Just thinking.

Compassion

My heart can be as hard as a rock sometimes. I believe it is a result of caring so much that sometimes I don't want the pain of feeling what others are going through. I want to sit in my little box and say, "I am sorry to hear that; pray, and God will work it all out," and be done with it. But I have come to realize that is not the compassion of Christ. I literally take on the pain and feelings of what others go through when they reveal their problems to me. It is not the greatest feeling, because I sit and ponder ways to help. But I realized that God allowed them to share their burdens with me so that I can pray for them, and when He tells me to, be used to help. Prayer is only one part of the Christian walk. Our actions should demonstrate the love that Christ shows us as well. I wonder, does Christ ever get tired of carrying my burdens? How would I feel if He just said, "Oh, sorry to hear that—try prayer," and left it at that? But Christ does not treat us this way. No, He listens and answers. No, we cannot help everyone in every situation. But by opening our hearts to the situations that others face, we are open to letting God use us in any way He sees fit. A hard heart may seemingly protect us from emotional pain, but it may cause another to suffer unnecessarily. Is your heart hardened to the trials and pains of others? If so, prepare to receive the same when you go through your own trials. I learned the hard way!

Just thinking.

More Than Fans

I will be the first to admit that I am a big fan of Christ. One may say, "Well, what's wrong with that?" Let's take a look. When we think of fans, we think of a person who admires, loves, promotes, enjoys, and, sometimes, is infatuated with a person (usually of celebrity status). The fan does not really know the person they are a fan of. They only know what they see or are told about this person. In most cases, they are left to admire from a distance. It is unlikely that they will ever meet the person face-to-face, and thus, their perspective of the person is limited. I have been, and still am, a fan of Christ. I speak highly to others of what He does and promote His works. I love and admire Him for who He is. But it has not been until recently that I realized that I have the opportunity to be more than a fan. I have the opportunity to be His friend. Check it out! When we can transcend from the position of fan to friend, our perspective is changed. Christ is no longer this "celebrity" that we desire to meet—not at all. He becomes the friend we have to keep! For a friend is one who we know, love, and have intimate contact with. Don't get me wrong, being a fan is a good start! However, a progressive faith walk is just that—*progressive*! And we must seek to know Christ on a more personal level. Who better to speak on the goodness and righteousness of a person's being than a close personal friend? So, friend or fan?

Just thinking.

Share the Struggle

The joy of the Lord, and His blessings and mercies that cover us are truly wonderful. But as followers of Christ, we are not promised to receive only good. We are "lambs for the slaughter" (Rom. 8:36). It is only by God's unchanging hand, and our faith in Him, that we can handle the hardships that we encounter. I have always been quick to tell others of all the wonderful things that God has done for me. But I don't often talk about the tough times, consequences of sin, or any hardships that I've experienced. I guess I felt that I should only focus on the good things. But God said *all* things work to the good for those that love Him (Rom. 8:28). Even the hardships are blessings. But more importantly, if others, who do not know Christ, only see us when we are at our best, then we give a false representation of what God is about. The Bible reveals Christ at His best and worst times in order to show the glory of God's will and serve as a testimony for believers. Hardships are testimonies that demonstrate the power of God to heal, save, bring us through, and make us whole again! I encourage you to not only share the blessings of Christ, but to also share (as the Holy Spirit directs you) the tough times that Christ has helped you to endure. We don't know what

others are going through and knowing that someone else is making it through the same thing they are struggling with may be the seed God needs planted at the time!
Just thinking.

Window Shopping

This is a concept that many can identify with: seeing things in a store that you know you can't get at the time, while in the back of your mind, you're imaging what you would do if you got it! Well, in my spiritual walk, I "window shop" as well. I see the things that God has for me, and look at them from a distance, thinking that I am not in a position to claim them at the time. But in the back of my mind, I imagine what it will be like when God does put me in position to acquire them. Things like diligence, stronger faith, a consistent prayer life, obedience, and the like. There is major difference though, and that is that in my spiritual walk, I have unlimited credit! Those spiritual things that I want, I have access to, even if I don't feel as if I can "afford" them at the moment. In our spiritual walk, faith is our currency, Christ is the cashier, and all that we desire we must simply ask for, with no concern of the price. It has been paid (Matt. 20:28)! I desire to be more like Christ, and I try, but it seems as though when I look up, I am still not in the position I feel I need to be in to acquire more of His traits. Hogwash! (LOL.) We are all works in progress, and if I base my spiritual growth on what I have at this point, I will never be in position (Heb. 11:1). Christ has paid the price for us to have unlimited access to His line of spiritual credit! What's in your wallet?

Just thinking.

Let 'Em Talk

I had the pleasure of seeing some old friends recently and it was a blessing. As we sat and recalled the days of old, I was reminded of how I used to be. I was an ill-tempered and erratic person. "Crazy," they called me. I can laugh about it now, but back then I was young and sensitive. See, I was the way I was because I felt that people would not accept me for who I truly was. So as a result, I developed a technique that allowed me to act like a fool in order to hide who I truly was. In retrospect, it was a sad sight. I lived as someone else so that people would not talk about me as being different. But the lie I lived caused them to think I was not just different, but crazy too! Then God showed me that the world would never accept who I am until I first accepted myself. I had to be shown that folks are going to talk about me regardless. If I do everything right, they will say, "He thinks he's better than us," or "He's always trying to show somebody up!" If I messed up everything, they would say, "What a f*ck up!" or "What is he thinking?" No matter what, people will talk; sadly, that is the nature of man. If they can't figure you out, they talk. If they think they have you figured out, they talk! Ironically, there is peace in this. Christ walked this earth, and I recall reading about people talking about Him like a dog (Matt. 27:27–44). He reminds us that if the world hates us, remember it hated Him first (John 15:18). I know I am nowhere close to where Christ was, and so why wouldn't they talk about me? The world is filled with talkers and critics that constantly have a word or two for us. The question is, "Are we listening to them, or are we listening to our God?"

Just thinking.

Our Self

I grew up in a home in which self was first and foremost. This is not a knock on my upbringing or my parents, it is simply the reality of how I was raised. I was taught that you take care of yourself first, and then help others if you can! However, I was always different. I used to get in trouble for giving away our food and other material things to those that I felt did not have enough. I would always open our doors to those that needed a place to stay or some help. This proved to be a problem, seeing as it was not my house or my things. This, I understood. But as I got older, and the Lord opened my eyes. He showed me that the spirit of wanting to help others is always going to create waves for those who are in the world. As Christians, we relinquish our rights to self. Although this is an ongoing and difficult process, it is part of who we now are. Christ put Himself last, if at all! What if He had thought of Himself first? Would He still have sacrificed His life so willingly? Pause and ask yourself, "Would I?" I know I cannot say that I would, but that is the level of selflessness I strive for. To forget about myself and be of service and of help to another. There is no greater joy than to have problems of you own and then be used, at the same time, to help someone else. We are Christians, not "Selftians," and so our walk should cause us each day to lose a little more of our self. Believe me, I am far from totally selfless, but if we all sacrifice a little more of our self each day, think of how much more God has to work with!

Just thinking.

The Dirty Room

When guests pop in unexpectedly, and I don't have a chance to clean, I just close the doors to those rooms that need to be cleaned. I think to myself, "If the door is closed, then they won't know that it's junky!" It's funny to me because the Holy Spirit revealed that this is also how I handle some of my spiritual rooms in my temple (life/body). I simply try to allow God to only move in those spaces where I think He would be pleased. The areas that need work are kept behind "closed doors." But then, I got a newsflash: God doesn't visit, instead He lives in us! I can't keep those doors shut forever. But unlike a guest, God wants us to open up those dirty rooms, simply so that He can clean them up. He is not impressed with what we consider to be "our best" (Isa. 64:6). He wants to see our worst so that He can show His best. So daily, I must ask the Lord to give me the courage to let Him in the "rooms" that I have dirtied up, so that He can clean them up. It's like this: Either I open the door now, or the Lord will knock it down later. I figure I'll save myself some unneeded "hinge" damage and let Him on in. How 'bout you?

Just thinking.

Throw Some Wood on the Fire

Have you ever seen a fire just as it's about to burn out? There's just enough heat to burn the existing wood, but the glow begins to hide under the accumulated ashes, so just enough heat to barely keep you warm. Well, recently I experienced the "fire fatigue." It was as if I was just going about the tasks that God had assigned me with a "it's my routine" mentality. It was sad! To think, here I was just going through the motions of serving, and not even realizing what a blessing it was to serve. My fire was dying out! Thank God for His word and the Holy Spirit's gentle, and sometimes very startling, reminders! These two things provided the kindling necessary to get my flame re-sparked! Sometimes, we may find ourselves in the midst of servitude and realize that our service has become mundane. It's not what we are doing, it's the spirit with which we are doing it (Eph. 6:7)! If we take a moment to remember who we are representing when we embark on a task, there is no way it becomes routine (Col. 3:23). So, if you ever find yourself in the midst of a "fire fatigue," please, oh please, don't question the task you have been given—question the spirit *you* give to it!

Just thinking.

Waiting in the Toolbox

I've sat for the past few days in turmoil over these messages. My intent was to keep writing over the past few weeks, but I was not allowed. I am not one for just saying anything when it comes to representing Christ. So, I prayed, asked for a word, and none was given. This put me in an uneasy state. Then, finally, it hit me—the perfect message. And as I sat to pray and type it, I heard the Holy Spirit say, "Not tonight!" I said, "But Lord, it came to me, it's good?" But again, "Not tonight! Wait till the morning." A lesson was learned. As much as I love sharing the Word, and as much of a blessing that I and others believe it to be, it means nothing without God's go ahead! He knows who it will reach and what purpose it will serve. The previous message cannot compare to this one. The test was: Will I obey His word, or do my thing? We are all just tools for His use, and we move when He says so—that means obeying. Think about tools for a minute. Hammers don't just get up and start banging. Chainsaws don't self-start and begin cutting wood. Screwdrivers don't come to life and start binding things (unless you live in a Disney movie or something). So, if we are tools, we must wait for the craftsman (God) to choose to use us. He knows which tools are needed for the divine task that He wants to complete. There can only be one craftsman in our lives. When we choose to change our roles (which we try to do at times—come on, I'm not the only one), then we end up trying to use the wrong tools for the situations we face. Are you a tool? Or have you taken on the role of a craftsman (1 Sam. 15:22)?

Just thinking.

Are You Willing to Wait?

In this crazy world, things move faster and faster each day. New technologies and gadgets allow for more efficient and speedier ways of completing tasks. Everyone seems in such a hurry to get things done. Correct me if I am wrong, but there seems to be an unofficial mandate to "get it while you can!" What happened to waiting? Many of us (myself included) bump our heads on the same doors over and over because we are not patient enough to wait on the Lord. If we never give Him the opportunity to make the path clear, then we are just setting ourselves up for the traps. Haste is not a characteristic of the Lord. When He tells us to move, then we move! But when we are directed to wait, we feel that we still have to do something to help the situation, and sadly we end up creating more confusion than before. Obedience is more honorable than sacrifice (1 Sam. 15:22). If He has told you to be still, then be still. But if He has directed you to go, then move with calculated quickness, for your instructions have been given. It's like a race; if you are the fastest person in the race, but you don't know where the finish line is, then how can you win (Isa. 40:31)?

Just thinking.

Don't Speak About It, Be About It

I'm always telling people how I love working with kids—like, for real! I love seeing their eyes light up when they learn something new, seeing the gratitude in their smile when you take time to listen to a problem they are having, and even seeing them finally "get it" and experience success. I love it all. But I left all of that! I left the teaching profession, believing in my mind, not my heart, that I was to do something else. I have many dreams and visions of what is to come in my life. It is as if God has shown me the destination but has not shown me fully how I will get there. But after much prayer and talking with my Brother and Father, I knew that it had to start with love. And I love teaching kids. The good, the bad, and the ugly aspects of it! So, I humbly returned this year to the classroom. To sit back and tell others, "Follow your heart and God will guide you from there" is hypocritical if I am not doing the same. I had to stop talking about what I want to do and love to do, and just do it (Prov. 14:23)! How God will use this to lead me to what He has for me, I don't know. That is the faith part (2 Cor. 5:7)! I am excited and amped for the challenges I am about to face! Not because I know what to do, but because I know who can do it! All this is to say that we have been given dreams and visions of where God wants us to be, but He does not always tell us in advance how we will get there. It takes daily faith and work (Prov. 16:9)!

Just thinking.

Why Me, Lord?

I am still sometimes surprised at how the Lord is using my hands to communicate these messages. I humbly say this because I recognize my faults daily and remember where I used to be. I can honestly say that, at first, I was not open to being used like this. I was so focused on my own situations that I did not realize what God was trying to use me for. Thank God for growth. So, I used to ask myself, "Why me?" I see so many people taking on pastoral positions and creating churches everywhere, and I thought, "You don't need me to say a word!" Then God showed me that He was using me anyway. "But why me?" I would still ask. I mean, I wasn't a total heathen (um . . . okay, depends on who you ask), but I had some very hedonistic characteristics! And I realized that was the reason (Eph. 4:24). A person who, in their own mind, can do no wrong or has done no wrong, cannot understand the ways of a public sinner. A public sinner is the person that does what he does in the open—contrary to the "behind the door" sinners, who project one image and perform another at home. My sin was open and bold (even after knowing the Lord, sadly) (Isa. 57:18-21). I'm not boasting, but when God changed these things in me, there was a noticeable difference in my walk and talk—this is my testimony. All this is to say, don't judge what God can do in your life by how you are right now. What He does may just be the tool He is using to change how you are! Often, as humans, we think that we have to get to a certain point for God to use us (Isa. 55:8–9). God will take the mess you are and use you to do mighty things. And as a result, it forces you to look at yourself, and allow Him to make changes in you! I stress that you should be encouraged and not resist what He is trying to do through you. It does not matter if *you* think you are not ready. He would not put you in this position if He thought that you weren't ready! We are all sinners, from the pulpit preacher to the parking lot pimp. And best believe God can use both, and any in between, to complete His perfect will (Acts 10:34).

Just thinking.

A Blessing Not Earned

In my past, I listened as people explained how they had done this and that, and as a result, God blessed them. Or because they did this, God did that. We are all subject to chance (Eccles. 9:2, 9:11–12). It is not by our own works that we are blessed. God does what He pleases in our lives and blesses whom He chooses (Rom. 9:18). In all actuality, if we look closely enough, both at the Word and our lives (Eph. 2:8–9), none of us are worthy of any of the blessings we receive. A blessing is a gift. Think about it! Do we earn gifts? No. When we humans give gifts, it is not always because a person did something. The best gifts come unexpectedly, and we appreciate them more because we know in our hearts that the giver did not have a "real" reason to give it. The greatest gift we ever received was being saved by Christ. I don't know about you, but I know that when I was saved, I did nothing to deserve that gift! All this is to say, if we think our actions are what causes God to bless us as He does, then we may need to get to know the Father a little better.

Just thinking.

Good Advice

A true friend will tell you when you are wrong. Also, they can be used to give good advice, if the Lord wills. Take, for instance, Job. When his friends came to visit, they sat quietly for a while before extending any words of advice. When they finally did, they said, "But as for me, I would seek God, and to God I would commit my cause" (Job 5:8). It goes without saying that we cannot always answer every question or concern of another, and often the best advice one can share with another is to take it to the Lord in prayer. We are not designed to be the solvers of every problem. No, we are just the tools that God uses to solve problems in His time. When I have friends that ask for it, I do find myself offering advice. But the best advice I have ever given was to pray over the situation. Job was in a tough spot—an extremely tough spot, to say the least. There was nothing his friends or family, what was left of them, could do for him. However, his true friend sent him to the one place where he knew his situation could be addressed: God! And lastly, he reminded Job of what God has and can do (Job 5:9–27)!

Just thinking.

The Gift That Keeps Giving

Some have been appointed to be teachers, some to be prophets, some to be apostles, and some to speak with varieties of tongues (1 Cor. 12:28–30). But Paul said that if there is no love along with the gift, then it is in vain (1 Cor. 13:1). One may ask, "Why is this important?" In this day and time, people are very impressionable. They are looking for indication of the presence of a higher power, and so the falsification of the gifts of the Holy Spirit can cause many to be led astray. Without love, there is no purpose in prophecy, because without love, the person is working under a different motive. Christ is a judge of motives (1 Cor. 4:5). "Acts of God" done with ill motives have led to many perishing—but Christ can see through them (Matt. 22:18). I want to encourage you to read and study 1 Corinthians for your own pleasure and knowledge. It reminds us that all that glitters ain't gold. The gifts that have been given to some mean nothing without love. "Love for what?" you might ask. Love for God and His people! What good is my gift if no one wants to get close enough to me for me to use it? Love begins with fear of God and ends with humility.

Just thinking.

Finally, I Cried

I remember the night that I cried out to the Lord for the first time. I was a drunk and high mess. As I drove down the street, I suddenly had a vision of all that I had been brought through in my life. The rebellion that had caused me to not believe in God, that had led me to trust in liquor and weed instead. I was a functioning addict. Then, that night, God just showed me in full color where I had been, and where I was headed if I kept this up. It was scary to see myself, in full color, doing what I thought was just having fun. As I drove, my eyes were on the road, but I was focused on the vision in my mind. I was being humbled! When I got home, I tried to pass it off as just trippin', but the Holy Spirit continued to allow me to see these things and ministered to my spirit. At last, I cried out to the Lord—I could not take it. As I did this, the floodgates of tears and concerns just opened, without me even thinking about it. I cried throughout the night and just asked for guidance. I recall this moment today, because I remind myself of where God has brought me from. We all have a past and things we are not proud of. We have all struggled in some shape, form, or fashion! And it is a beautiful thing to see where He has raised us up from. But we must not forget where we have been brought from, and the works of good God has performed in our lives (Ps. 77). We are all sinners, saved by grace, and recalling what God has brought us through is what keeps us humbled.

Just thinking.

Training Day

Children come out of the womb ready to be taught. They watch and learn from the people around them. Most of what they do is a learned behavior—from walking, to that little foul mouth in some cases (later, God pulls out what He placed in them)! Anyway, we are reminded to train up a child in the way that they are to go, and they will remember and utilize it when they get older (Prov. 22:6). Do we really train our children? Sit and think about it before you answer. With all the financial burdens of supporting a family, it has become tougher and tougher to spend any time with our children—let alone quality time. So, our daily habits and movements become the training mechanism for our children today. Oh yeah, they are watching us more than listening to us. We all notice daily the drastic change in our youth and we often sit back and wonder what has gone wrong. We contemplate every avenue of blame other than the one we actually have control over—ourselves. If we don't teach them what they need to know, who will? We feed them athletically (oh, little Johnny makes it to practice, don't he?), educationally (we tell them to study, study, and get good grades), and socially (5th graders with cell phones—don't lie, yours has one too!), but what about spiritually? Are we teaching them about the God we serve? If we think that going to church is the answer, we are mistaken. That is only one part of the equation. Our children are watching us for their daily training. How we speak, deal with others, handle situations, take time out for God, and so forth. The children of Israel lost connection with the God of their fathers and look at the trouble it caused them (Judg. 2:11–15). Either we make time for our children or the enemy will surely make time for them. Our current generation has lost connection with the true and living God. We sing His songs, but are we walking His walk daily? Remember, our habits of today are the next generation's habits of tomorrow; they are watching!

Just thinking.

P.S. For more, try Psalms 78.

Temptations

No, I don't mean the group. I'm talking about the temptation to sin. I have often heard people say that the Lord is testing them when they are face-to-face with a temptation. For instance, a sex addict who comes face-to-face with a person ready to jump in bed with them. According to some, this is the Lord testing the person's heart. But be assured that the Lord does no such thing. We are tempted when we focus on our own desires (James 1:13–16). Who can tempt God with evil? Nothing and nobody! When we are face-to-face with a temptation, it is a chance for us to repent of the evil desires that dwell in us. Oh, it ain't the easiest thing in the world to do, but it can be done. It must be clear who is doing the tempting. If we don't know the source of something, how can we address it? Imagine thinking that the Lord is tempting you and you are asking "Why?" That's like getting a cell phone bill and calling the water company to inquire about the high bill. What can they do about it? The enemy is a master at his tricks, and one of them is letting us believe that God is placing evil before us to see if we can pass the test. Be of good courage. We are all tempted by something, and it is only by the grace of God that we can turn away from it (James 4:7). But we have to recognize that our desires are the source of the temptations. Open up and let God get to the source of the problem!

Just thinking.

Faith Quiz

Our tasks are simple: have faith in the Lord Jesus Christ and walk accordingly. But how can we have faith? With so much destruction, chaos, and poverty, how can we have faith? With all the opportunity to focus on the wrong things, how can we have faith? With so many false prophets, priests, and preachers, how can we have faith? Paul said, "So then faith comes by hearing and hearing by the Word of God" (Rom. 10:17). Are you tuned in? When we hear the Word of God, it strengthens our faith in God. But if we are not tuned in to the Word, we miss it and we are weakened. For example, if you were a student in a math class, and the teacher said that the class was going to have a pop quiz, immediately the class would go into an uproar and not hear the teacher indicate that they are giving all the answers to the quiz during a brief review. So, while everyone is complaining about not being prepared, those that took time to listen closely would no doubt have the peace of mind for the upcoming quiz. Their faith in passing the test is based on what they heard, not on their ability. But for those that were complaining, couldn't hear what the teacher was saying, and thus feel at a loss, have no hope in passing. Are we listening to the teacher, gaining hope and faith, or are we in the back complaining and missing all the answers?

Just thinking.

The Enemy We Hate to Love

I am not into politics at all. But it is obvious that our nation, in general, is not pleased with the current administration. However misguided this administration is, and how evil we may feel their agenda is, it is still our duty to pray for and love them (Matt. 5:43–48). It is easy to sit back and say what we should, could, or would have done, but until you have experienced it, you don't know. God has *allowed* that administration to be there for a reason. Are we willing to be as forgiving as Christ was when He said, "Father forgive them for they know not what they do"? Man is flawed, and it is easy to like a person who does everything right, but our true test is dealing with the evil that is placed before us and treating our enemies with love and kindness! No, no, you don't have to send fresh pies and cakes to the White House or get-well cards for their mental illnesses (LOL). Simply pray for God's will to be done and think before we speak. If we sit back and judge, what makes us any different from them? Evil is evil, right?

Just thinking.

Where Is the Fear?

A child feels that a loving parent will do nothing to harm them. Even when that little leg is tapped or punishment is given, that child still comes to that parent for protection and love. The punishments create a sense of respect and fear in the child. Before they make a move (or usually it is after they make it, LOL) they think about the trouble they could be in. I used to think to myself, "My father is going to kill me!" And some of the punishments I got . . . For a moment, I thought I was close to death. But nonetheless, I knew that my father loved me, and I still went to him when I needed something. I feared his wrath and tried not to go too far to provoke it. Knowing that God is our Heavenly Father, where is the fear and respect for what He dislikes and despises? His mercy is so great that often we forget the fact that He is capable of punishment (Heb. 12:6). I hated the punishments that I got, but if I had not gotten them, Lord knows what I would have gotten into. The same with the Lord. Yes, His mercy is plentiful, but if you never get a punishment then you do not know His love (Heb. 12:7)! Many of us want to be closer to God and understand His ways. Solomon advised that until we respect and *fear* the Lord, we cannot begin to have knowledge (Prov. 1:7). The Lord, similarly, to any parent, only wants what's best for us. He knows, better than anyone, that if His child does not fear Him, then they will do what they please with no fear of punishment—which leads to having a spoiled brat! God's love is not just demonstrated by His blessings, but also by His correction (Heb. 12:6).

Just thinking.

Living the Life, or a Lifestyle?

In my youth, I always dreamed of being rich. I dreamed of millions and millions that I would benefit from and share with others. It was simple to me—I would use the gifts given to me and work to get rich! But thank God for a little understanding and His wisdom! Getting rich is not the end for Christians, if we really stop and think. Yes, our Father answers prayers according to His riches and glory, but He also checks the motives for which our prayers are asked! If we are asking to be prosperous for the sake of having the finer things in life, then what makes us any different from the world (Rom. 12:2)? The world searches for material and monetary gain in order to satisfy themselves. But we are warned that when we set our minds and hearts on these things we will never be satisfied (Eccles. 5:10–12). We end up like the silly donkey who, led by the carrot because of greed, finally reaches the destination of "success," only for that carrot to not be enough to satisfy after the long journey—and thus sets off again for more! To each his own. But as followers, we have to be mindful of the example we set for those watching us! If we pursue the same ends as they do "in the name of

Jesus," we demonstrate that God is no more than an ATM at our disposal! If we simply focus on the purposes that God has placed in our hearts to pursue, we don't have to worry about having enough (2 Cor. 9:6–11). Are we trying to live the Christian life, or a worldly lifestyle?

Just thinking.

An Enjoyer

Take a second, minute, hour, day, week, or whatever you like, and enjoy the blessing of life! A lot of us are so caught up in doing "something" that we forget that God has blessed us with the gift of life. We are encouraged to appreciate the blessings of each day that we are given by the preacher (David's son) in Ecclesiastes 3:9–14. If all of our moments are spent in labor, when do we ever get a chance to stop and appreciate what God has blessed us with? I understand that these are hard and financially troubling times, but rest assured—no matter how much we work and store up, it is all in vain if we never stop and enjoy the blessings of our labors! Life is short—ask any "older" person. They'll tell you that it seemed like just yesterday they were doing their thing, and then one day they woke up and they were older! Be encouraged and know that what will be, shall be, and Christ is in control of it all! Be a good laborer, and an enjoyer of the benefits of that labor as well. God gave it, so enjoy it!

Just thinking.

P.S. For more, try Proverbs 23:4–5.

Travel Plans

We do not know His will for our lives other than what the Bible has indicated: unspeakable joy, peace, prosperity (it does not say money, but *prosperity*), and unconditional love. God speaks dreams, destinies, and goals to each of us, but often does not reveal the details of how we will get there. This is the faith part. We have to trust Him that we will get there. As we go to Him daily and ask what is to be done, each day guides us closer to His will for our lives. We often mistake our own plans for our lives as God's will for our life. We become frustrated or disappointed (I speak from experience) when it does not go the way we planned (John 13:7). But He told us that we will not understand His ways or plans for our lives. Think about it: When we plan trips we map them out, make reservations, and pack accordingly, because we know exactly where we are going and how we are getting there. But how in the world can we plan for a destination when we don't know the path we have to take? No one but God knows the who, what, when, where, and why of our journey. So, we have a choice: we can sit back and enjoy the ride, or drive ourselves crazy trying to get there on our own—which, sadly, we will not do anyway (we can't get to a Godly destination without God, LOL). We are destined for the greatness that God has for us, and if we just trust in Him, we will get there, in *His* time.

Just thinking.

We Ain't Seeing Clearly

It is our duty as Christians to be an example and to help others see the way. However, Christ strongly warned us about the temptation of hypocrisy (Matt. 7:1–5). He used the example of the speck in our brother's eye and the beam in ours! The best example of witnessing and spreading God's Word is our daily life. When folks see the changes God makes in us, we are being used to witness. Too often, we (as always, I'm including myself) try to tell others what they are doing wrong and witness to them. Although the intent is good, we end up focusing more on trying to change them (which only Christ can do anyway) than changing our own ways (1 Cor. 3:7). For example, if I talk to my students and tell them that they need to watch their mouths and work on their attitude, but then every time they get on my nerves I explode in anger and curses, what good are the words I spoke to them earlier? Or how about if I tell my children to clean their rooms, and they see a mess in mine each day? Or lastly, I tell my wife to respect me and listen to what I say, and then I never consider her words when she speaks. It all boils down to practicing what we preach, and it is easier when we let our actions do the preaching. Focusing on changing others blinds us to our own issues, which turns into the blind leading the blind (Luke 6:39).

Just thinking.

I Love God More

When a person that we don't care about offends us, we can usually shake it off. In our minds, we think, "They must be crazy or something!" But when it is family or someone we love, it becomes a lot harder to deal with. Christ warned that our enemies will be those of our own household (Matt.10:35–37). Now, I did not understand this at first, because I was like, "Nah, my folks love me!" But then I asked for understanding. God comes first (Prov. 3:6)! Anyone who goes against this is an enemy of the faith. It may sound extreme, but there is no gray area when it comes to God. The reason family is so easily used as an enemy is because of the very bond of emotion that ties them to us—the same bond that caused us to flinch a little when we received this message! We live and die for Christ, not man. Family and friends can easily lead us astray, if with good intent (Eve, Lot's wife, etc.). Be mindful, watch and pray (Matt. 26:41). This does not mean to isolate yourself from them, unless instructed to, but to keep your service to Christ at the forefront of your life, and it will be fine. I believe that is also why He said, "But I tell you: Love your enemies and pray for those who persecute you," (Matt. 5:44). Be encouraged by truth and service to Christ. Only God knows His plan for you, so put Him first and things will fall in line (Rom. 8:28).

Just thinking.

Don't Look Like No Saint

If you were walking down the street and passed by a homeless person who was speaking from the Bible, would you stop and listen? If he were asking for donations from those that passed by, would you contribute? How about if you were walking and saw a man with nice clothes, beautiful pamphlets, flyers, and brochures proclaiming the Word of God—would you take one and listen? And if he were asking for donations, as he explained and showed the various programs that the funds would be used for, would you contribute? For earthly reasons, we often go by what we see with our eyes (2 Cor. 5:7). If a man is dressed in fine clothes and preaching the gospel, we assume that God is taking care of His own. But, often, when the same gospel is preached by a person of low economic status, we assume that he is crazy, or just hustling and begging. The greatest teacher or preacher that ever walked this earth, walked humbly with nowhere to lay His head (from birth, remember?), and He forced those that He taught, just by His presence, to get past the appearance. As the old folks say, "Everything that glitters, ain't gold!" Check out James 2:1–10.

Just thinking.

Sharing

Sharing what God has done for me, and what He has shown me, is peace. I don't share so that people will say, "Oh, he is wise, he knows something." I truly understand only one thing: I understand little in this life. Each day is a new learning experience that strengthens me for the road ahead, and it is only through God's humility that I realized this (Prov. 9:10). If left to my own understanding, I would probably be so self-involved that I would not see the things which God shows me. I share because in my heart I know that God wants to use us all. If He wants to use me to encourage and uplift, then I will do it gratefully. I have looked back over some of the previous writings and wondered how they might have been received. Then peace is given in knowing that "truth is truth." It may not be what we would like to see or hear, but it is truth. I accept the truth of both my good and bad aspects. Transparency is a means of helping another avoid the same snares I have succumbed to. I pray that each writing received is filled with the love I have for My Father, and that someone may be blessed. Yes, this message is about sharing! If I don't share with love, then I am not sharing at all (1 Cor. 16:14). I would be giving out of obligation, which would eventually turn to resentment when nothing is given in return. So, I asked myself, "Why am I giving—so I can get back, or so that others may be blessed?

Just thinking.

Church Today?

Now more than ever, we are seeing a boom in the world of religion. There are bigger congregations and churches, and many people are being drawn to God. To God be the glory. But let us not forget that "church" isn't a building; it's a state of heart, spirit, and mind (Matt. 16:15). We, each one of us, is the church, for Christ dwells in each one of us, constantly drawing others by His spirit (1 Timothy 5). I wondered why folks would come to me for advice and with concerns, even though I was younger, or even inexperienced with the subject they were dealing with. It took a while (a long while), before I realized that they were *not* drawn to me because of what I knew, but because of the spirit of God that dwelled in me. Daily we "gotsta" (as the old folks say, LOL) have service, if only for a while, because we never know when someone will come to our "church doors" looking for help. Will we be ready to receive them, as we would on Sunday? As the pastors say, "The doors of the church are now open!" Each morning, if we open the doors of our hearts, He will draw all men unto His "church" (John 12:32).

Just thinking.

Message for Me

Have you ever been to church when the pastor delivers a message that is seemingly perfect for a person you know? Or someone gives you advice, and as soon as you hear it you think, "They should hear this!" Yeah, me too! It seems so perfect; God sends a message to us, through someone else, and we deliver it to the person we think needs to hear it. We are God's vessels, right? But that is usually not the case. Think back to the telephone game as a child. We would stand in a line and pass down a message, from one ear to another. If the message was the same at the end of the line as it was when it was first said, the team wins. If it was different, the team lost! It was always easier when there were less people in the line, because the more people in the line, the more difficult it was to keep the original message! You are smiling right now because you see where this is headed (LOL)! God does use people to share a word with us (Mark 16:15), but for most, it is rare when He shares a word through someone else to pass it on to another. Usually, the very message that we believe is for the next person is for us! The less people involved in the relaying of the message, the more likely it is to get delivered correctly. So now, when I hear a message that seems great for a friend or relative, I am very conscious about asking who it is for. Often

God reveals how it applies to me. We each have a direct line to Christ, and He came so we wouldn't have to hear what He wants to tell us through the "grapevine." Because the Lord knows that by the time the message gets to who needs it, it's very different than what He sent out (Deut. 4:36)!

Just thinking.

Trying Times

Change happens and we all (believers and non-believers) face trying situations. The only and most important difference is that, as believers, we are in possession of all the tools needed to withstand and overcome the trials. The most important tool is faith. It was never said to us that we would experience only good in our lives once we accepted Christ as our savior (Ps. 86:7). On the contrary, once we accepted Him, we put a big target on our chest that says, "I believe!" (Job 7:20). And the enemy said, "Oh, you believe, do you?" (1 Pet. 5:8). We are tested daily, and it is only by faith that we can endure (Heb. 10:32–39). Be encouraged when adversity comes your way. It usually comes when you are attempting to do what God has asked of you (see the entire book of Job)! Be strong and press on. And when you make it through, give thanks for faith (James 1:2, 1:12). We are here to encourage one another. I encourage you, as God encourages me.

Just thinking.

Too Righteous?

Can one be too righteous? I believe so (Eccles. 7:16–18). Have you ever been around a person that is so righteous that they seem vain? You know—when someone else does something wrong, they are quick to point it out and harp on it. Constantly hitting whoever they meet, with quotes and scriptures; it's almost as if the Word is all they know, and anyone who does not see it their way is lost. I can recall a time in my life when I was that person. I was self-righteous. But through humility and patience, God opened my eyes to true understanding. I look at Christ: He never went out proclaiming how righteous He was. His actions convinced the people. He didn't quote the Bible without cease. He actually spoke the principles of the Bible in a way that the people could relate to (Matt. 13:34). He was able to do this because the words were written in His heart, and not just being read from a page. An overly righteous person sits on the hill and yells out what must be done. A servant of God goes down into the valley and shows how it can be done. An overly righteous person sits on the hill with others and condemns what they see. A servant of God goes into the valley and shows people a different way. I had to ask myself, "Am I righteous or am I a servant?" and "Am I humble enough to go where there is no light and let God shine through me?" (This little light of mine.) Or will I sit on the hills and shake my head in shame as the people perish?

Just thinking.

BE ENCOURAGED ON THIS DAY

Many of us are facing trying situations, and Lord knows you are about at your wits' end. But please be encouraged. We are living in times in which it is so easy to lose focus on what's really important. First and foremost, what God shows and gives us is most important. An endless supply of provision, guidance, care, patience, understanding, and love! These situations that we face are simply distractions to get our minds away from this fact (Mark 4:19). There is nothing in this world worth losing the love God has for us (Mark 8:36). We are in times in which financial security and prosperity are being stressed, even by Christians. However, if we are to be examples of how Christ was, then how can prosperity be our focus (Heb. 13:5)? Finances are important, but are they to be the first priority? There is more to life than the obvious daily rat race and struggle, believe it or not. So, for those of us facing situations that seem to be destroying our faith, strength, and courage, I encourage you to grab hold of the peace and strength of God (Ps. 34:17)! Be sure that *all* things are working to the good for those that love Him! Do not be consumed by the haters that try to make you focus on the "reality" of what you face. For we live by faith—trusting what God has said, not what the world has shown (2 Cor. 5:7)! Lastly, and most importantly, ask God for help! No, really ask Him. While we have been sitting trying to figure it all out, God has been waiting for us to give it to Him and let it go (Ps. 55:22). Be encouraged and keep the faith!

Just thinking.

Calorie Counting

If I don't fill up on encouragement, wisdom, love, understanding, and the like, then what will I have to give to others? I have seen the results of myself being filled with evil as well as good. As a youngster I was filled, daily, with evil (trying to fit in) and that is what I gave out (Matt. 15:19). As a result, I got back what I gave out. As a youngster, I spoke with hatred, anger, and frustration, and wondered why people reacted to me the way they did. As the saying goes, "You are what you eat." That applies to spiritual food as well. If one feeds on the misfortune of others, on hatred and contempt for others, selfishness, anger from past or present events, and the like in order to make themselves feel better, then that person becomes consumed by these things, and eventually the negatives become their personal attributes (Gal. 6:7). Thank God for Mercy! When I learned to feed on the Word of God, wisdom, understanding, and love became my attributes (Jer. 10:12). I had a healthier spiritual diet. We are what we take in, good or bad! And we can only give what we have inside! See the connection? In today's society there is a heavy petition for us to be in better physical shape—watching our weight and what and how much we eat. I ask you, and myself, are we watching our spiritual intake as much as our physical intake?

Just thinking.

Confirmation

I don't know it all. Frankly speaking, I don't know much of anything. I admit it! I am not as wise as I thought and not as smart as I lead myself to believe. I say this not to put myself down, but as a confession of arrogance. At one point, I depended on my knowledge and understanding of things in order to make decisions and help others (Dan. 11:33). What a mistake that was! My understanding and knowledge are limited (1 Cor. 3:19). "There is a way that seems right to a man, but its end is the way of death" (Prov. 16:25). God encourages us to seek wise counsel, which first comes from Him and His Son (Prov. 9:10, 12:15). He also places people in our lives that have wisdom, and we should adhere to that wisdom according to what He has told us; truth is always confirmed (2 Cor. 13:1). If we knew how to handle every situation and had the answers to every problem, then why would we need God? I encourage you to stop and ask yourself, "Who am I depending on for understanding, myself or God?" I am learning the hard way. I pray you can learn from my mistakes and avoid some unwanted bumps and bruises!

Just thinking.

God Loves You

Really! At times we hear this so much that we forget to take time to think about or appreciate what it truly means. The love that is shown to us is unconditional. It is not based on how we act or what we do (Rom. 5:8). When we mess up, He loves us. When we do right, He loves us. Often it is our own inability to love ourselves that hinders us. We'll say to ourselves, "I really f*cked that up! I know God is mad at that!" or "I know God forgives, but I don't know about this one!" I know in my heart I am not the only one who has had these discussions. But I share this testimony. No matter what it is, God will forgive, and He still loves us (Ps. 86:15)! If you take a look at the Bible you will see stories of killers, adulterers, fornicators, liars, thieves, and others who God loved so much that He allowed their lives to be changed over time, so that they may serve Him (1 Sam. 12:19–25). Love that is unconditional is hard to imagine because, as humans, we put a limit on how long and how much we will love someone. I offer this last word of encouragement: God is not human, and His love is not limited (Ps. 107:8–9)!

Just thinking.

Feeling or Faith?

Honestly, I didn't feel like writing this message. I was so focused on the issues in my own life that I did not feel that I could be used to inspire anyone. How can I encourage anyone when I am not encouraged myself? I did not *feel* like it! But what if God—and Jesus, for that matter—moved by their feelings? Did Christ *feel* like dying for our sins? Does God *feel* like saving us from our continual disobedience? If we only moved based on feeling, we would miss out on a lot of God's blessings. If you don't feel like doing something—whether it is for someone else or yourself—just ask yourself, "Do I live by faith or feelings?"

Just thinking.

Got Patience?

In today's society, patience is a rare concept. Instant gratification and reward are an underlying theme of today's lifestyle. Instant everything—from loans to health cures! What ever happened to patience? It may be human nature to want what we want, when we want it, but it has been proven that things acquired in haste are often bigger burdens than blessings. What's our hurry? That doggone Darwin, survival of the fittest, and the competitive nature of our society foster a need for us to "get it while the getting's good!" But God works differently. He knows that if we get something before we are ready, we will more than likely not appreciate it, ultimately abuse it, and lose it (Matt. 6:8; Matt. 25:14–30). I had to ask myself, "What's my rush?" Is it better to move slowly and be sure, or move quickly and doubt the steps taken? Ask for guidance and "wait, wait I say on the Lord" (Ps. 27:14)! Good things come to those that wait (Lam. 3:25).

Just thinking.

MERCY

In the words of Marvin, "Mercy, mercy [on] me." This is one attribute that I am thankful that God possesses (Eph. 2:4; Titus 3:5). Without it, where would I be? It is a large misconception that once Christ enters your life, sinning stops (1 John 1:8–10). Some even go as far as to convince you that if you do sin then there is no way that Christ is in you. Hogwash! If this were so, then our Heavenly Father would have no need for the aforementioned attribute (Ps. 86:5). I saw a sign once that read, "A saint is a sinner that keeps trying." We all sin, and do not be fooled into thinking that one is greater than another. Mercy allows us to go before the throne of grace and ask for forgiveness (Titus 3:5). Really, the toughest part of it all is forgiving yourself! God's attribute of mercy also helps with self-condemnation.

Just thinking.

Stress?

One of the deadliest diseases is stress because we have been conditioned to believe that it is a part of being busy. Can we agree that Christ was a busy man? Walking daily amongst the poor in spirit, battling the upper class' perceived understanding of salvation, etc. Whew, just thinking about it makes me stressed! I do not believe that this stressed Him out. He utilized his connection to God to deal with the pressures of these tasks. So, if Christ, in all his perfection, needed God to help with the stress of his burdens, then what makes us think we do not need the same (Mark 6:31–32)? Ask for healing of the disease that quietly kills our hopes, dreams, joy, patience, home life, and relationships (Ps. 94:19). God simply asks that we give Him our burdens and take His (Matt. 11:29–30). Oh, it is a task, but practice makes us better, though not perfect. If you think you may be stressed, guess what? You probably are. Don't delay, give it to Your Father! His burdens are light.

Just thinking.

One Day at a Time

It always sounds so simple, and really, it is. We just have a way of making it difficult. Be encouraged and know that all is working for your good. Take five minutes out of your day and just think back to where you were five years ago. The type of person you were, the things you did, the thoughts you had, the troubles you faced, and then look at where God has brought you to (Ps. 113:6–8). Oh, I had to laugh when I thought back (and many of my friends know why)! But it is encouraging to know that what is now, will not always be! We are all works in progress (Phil. 2:13)!

Just thinking.

A Moment

There is hope in today. Do not fret over tomorrow or what happened the day before (Matt. 6:34). Take the opportunity that is today and have hope that all is working for your good (Rom. 8:28). Do not complicate the day by entertaining thoughts of things you have no control over (Luke 12:22–26)! Let each hindrance become a hurdle, and each trouble become a testimony for what God is doing in your life. Be encouraged on this day that all is well, even though our physical eye may see different—that is why we are told to walk by faith (2 Cor. 5:7). Take ten minutes out of your day (a moment) and just give thanks for the good and the bad (1 Thess. 5:16–18). Witness to yourself for the strength to appreciate the good, and the strength to press on through the bad.

Just thinking.

Power

With each new dawning that we are blessed to see, we have the opportunity to either share hope and light with others or despair and darkness (Prov. 18:21). I pray that you choose the former. Christ strengthens us to share love when we are feeling anger, to smile when a frown is all we have, to laugh when our situations say we should cry, and to be peaceful when violence and anger seem like the only paths to take (2 Thess. 3:16). Take a moment and think. What are you sharing with others today?

Just thinking.

POETRY

All in the Letter

Written so power could flow
Father's spirit is too much for most
His prophets put it to paper
Faith?
In it?
Test to see
God—not me
Read and studied
My heart knows God loves me
Qualified
Jesus died
For our sins
Strive to be complete
He is strong when we are weak
Honorably sing praises and hymns
Till God calls all men
Brother lives in thee
Christ resurrected in me
You
Truth, we speak
All of the Father
Told us many times

But we cast it out of our minds
He sent a letter
We understand better
Than His prophets' stern words
Lies absurd
Do no evil
When we fall short
God's the support
We need
Holy kiss to greet
The saints
To God, give thanks
Grace of the Brother
Love of the Father
Communion of the Spirit
Be with us till He writes again
Scriptures in the hearts of all men
All this in a letter

Based on 2 Corinthians 13:5–14

Approaching Fast

The child must go without
The fast loosens bonds and relieves heavy burdens
The peace of the fast is quickly approaching
(No joking)
Fast is here
Oppressed, go free
Every yoke loosened
Thine bread shared with the hungry
Given with a humble heart
Time of fast
Things come to pass
Light breaks forth
Lord protects me
Call to God
"Here I *am*"
Removing wickedness
Is true bliss
Through the fire
Made pure gold
Not in vain
God makes a change
Not the same

DR. CHARLES A. GUILFORD, III

Afterward
After Word
Myself, to the hungry and afflicted soul
God in control
He does
Satisfy!
Approaching fast—this fast
Watered garden
Land flower
Waters will not fail
When the fast has passed
Bonds will not last
Laugh with joy
No longer bound
The Repairer of the breach
The Restorer of the streets
Used to keep up foundations
In the fast way

Based on Isaiah 58:6–12

Church Announcements

He saw her in a vision on a Sunday afternoon
The sun was shining brightly, but he could still see the moon
As he walked to his car, he saw his reflection in the mirror
And a ghostly figure behind him he wished he could see clearer
He opened the door and slid into the seat
He had just cast off all of the burdens he'd acquired this past week
He said a silent prayer and started up the car
And then he set the radio station to WHUR
He checked the mirror to his right and the one on his side of the door
But when he checked the rearview mirror, he saw the ghostly figure once more
This time it was clearer; he could see it was a woman
But he had no clue as to why in his mirrors she was looming
Her face was brown, the smoothest complexion he had ever seen
And she wore the angel's garment, including halo and wings
Long dark-brown hair with a smile of gold
She possessed the type of beauty that can never grow old
He blinked his eyes once and she was no longer there
He wondered, was he dreaming, and began to get scared

When he arrived home, he went straight upstairs
He had to make it to the bedroom—he knew he needed prayer
He called out to Jesus and fell to his knees
He closed his eyes tightly and soon felt at peace
He said, "Lord, who is this woman I have seen?
Was it a vision from you or was it just a dream?"
God said, "Listen, I know how you feel
And I will be the first to tell you this woman is real."
He asked, "But who is she, what purpose will she serve?
Is she going to teach me how to live and stand on your Word?"
God laughed at his innocence and replied in a light-hearted tone,
"No, my son, she is the one you can call your own
Your wife to be is this woman that you see in your vision
She is a reward for your trust in God and your faithful living!"
He smiled and joy filled his heart, for he knew he didn't deserve it
But he had walked by faith, kept himself pure and he saw it was worth it
God said, "My son you have served me with your heart, and I know what you desire.
I have placed a love in this woman's heart that will burn like eternal fire.
She has all that you need and even the things your body craves,
She will be my blessing to you, love her with your heart all of your days."
He replied, "When will I meet her? Will I run into her soon?
Or is this a test of my patience and I have to wait a thousand moons?"
God laughed and said, "Soon, soon you will connect, and the love will be sparked
And if you ground your love in me, you two shall never part."
He thanked the Lord for taking the time to help him out
He stood up with peace in his heart and free from all doubt

Three Sundays later, as he sat in the back of the church
He was thinking of the week ahead and how he had so much work
The pastor had preached, and the choir was about to sing
So he closed his eyes to get the fullness of the joy the song would bring
The piano began to play, followed by the bass
They were singing a song about Jesus and his amazing grace
Then a voice like that of an angel started singing alone
He wondered whose sweet voice was coming from the microphone
He opened his eyes and looked towards the front of the church
And saw the most beautiful woman, to him, put on this earth
A tear streamed down his cheek and he could barely catch his breath
It was the woman from his vision standing on stage, in the flesh
As she sang, with each note he felt her voice caress his skin
And he hoped she would at no time soon bring the song to an end
They made eye contact and exchanged simple smiles
And for a second, a brief moment, he felt like a child
Before she could finish, the Spirit rushed through his heart
And he found that he couldn't wait until she finished her part
He went to the front of the church to let the world know
He had just received a blessing from God, his appreciation he had to show
He said, "This woman I have seen before in a vision given by God.
She was sent to be my wife and I know this may sound odd.
However, this announcement is only meant for her soul,
If you let me, I will love you now until our bodies become old.
I will treat you like the angel you are—a perfect gift from above.
I will embrace you in my arms and with my heart give you eternal love."
The congregation was in awe, and a silence fell over the church

In his heart he prayed that the words he used would work
Then a single clap from a member turned into a cheer
And the woman from the vision also shed a tear
They embraced at the altar and both walked away
To enjoy each other's company, and together they would pray
As church let out, there was a buzz about the things that'd happened
Everyone was trying to figure out exactly who started the clapping
Mrs. Adams said, "It was I who started the celebration.
I thank God for the love in that man's heart; he showed true determination.
Besides, in my eighty-six years of hearing God's Word,
Those were the best church announcements I have ever heard!"

Based on Proverbs 18:22

Commands for the Future

Fathers, stubborn and rebellious
No regard for commands
Not the plan
Jacob receives rules
Generations not to mimic fools
Given to a land
Fathers to take commandments in hand
Pass to future generations
No hesitation
Parables made it clear to them
A new legacy begins
The future would know of the God they serve
The fathers must spread the word
Generation to generation
Word passed
God would shelter through storms
Wonderful works He has done
Stubborn, so He sent His son
So youth never forgets
God commanded it

Elders should teach
Commands given to Jacob's heart
Not faithful to the Lord
Stubborn ways
Not fair
Children would never make it there
The Secret Place
To see God's grace
Commands for the future were sent
Teach children to repent
Wonders of the Lord
Commands ignored
Generations to come
More rebellious than previous ones
Instructions retrieved
God sent what we need
Commands for the future
"Teach my ways"
Experience brighter days
Unlike rebellious fathers
Speak this to the generations to come
"This I command"

Based on Psalm 78:4–8

Hate On, World

Tears flow
A change
Christ in my heart and soul
Not physical—Spiritual
Different from the worldly man
His eyes full of spite
God has done for me
Brother already warned
"The world will hate you, but they hated me first"
The world not of
World show me love?
Who don't know God's Word
A coward with nerve
I AM has given
My mission
Hated the perfect one
God's Son
Me?
Hate received
Not accepted
Rejected
Pray for souls

DR. CHARLES A. GUILFORD, III

They know not what they do
World, hate on
Guided through storms
He who sent me
His word at heart
Will understand my part
God loves through them
Not worldly women and men
Preachy words
"Don't hate the haters, it clouds your judgement"
Hated Brother first
Much worse
Persecution
Peace
In a world that will hate on

Based on John 15:18–21

Her Rewards

She brings happiness to all that find her
Who have the power to understand
Greater than fine materials of earth
Our desires cannot compare to her worth
Sent by the Father to lengthen the days
Peace to all who embrace her ways
She is the future and the past
The hope of knowledge, yet much greater
Her presence, peace
her way, pleasant
Jewels nor gems satisfy men, like she
Giving man peace
Adding days to life
The only way to truth, is she
Understanding placed in man's hands
Only through her
Many rewards
God made it so
Happy are all who embrace her and her ways
No games played
Embrace the tree of life
Keep her in your heart

From now until our Father returns
The only lady needed by all
With her you will not fall
She knows all
Happy is the man who finds wisdom
Who embraces the blessings of understanding
Her rewards are far greater than the heart's desire
Dream not of all that can be received
But of the path that she will eventually lead
You down
Her sound, peace
God's peace of mind
She is fine, and found
In the presence of God
Seek her now, and find out her ways
So that you will have brighter days
Peace be to him who attains her

Based on Proverbs 3:13–18

Like Solomon Prayed

Time has come
Require peace
Solomon prayed for an understanding heart
Granted
Wisdom planted
Roots of the tree
For all to see
Not himself that he desired of
Blessings, described as love
His father too—same position
Son knew God's wisdom and understanding were missing
From honor a king receives
Solomon kneeled, prayed, rose, believed
Never before
God answered prayers
Removed worries and cares
Simply asked
As his kingship passed
Keep the statutes, ways, commandments
Riches of the Father sent
Extra days for his life
Son walks in his Father's light

DR. CHARLES A. GUILFORD, III

People would soon see
God's understanding
Dance like David to give God praise
Pray like Solomon prayed
God give us understanding hearts

Based on 1 Kings 3:6–14

LOVED AND CHASTENED

He is the Father
Spirit of truth
Moves Heaven and Earth
So then
Most men
Reveal no evil
He knows
He must
Chasten us
Love, He gives
Is too much with us?
We look at it
Take it for granted
Evil is planted
Means of rebuke
Nothing but truth
Can we see?
He loves you and me
Be zealous and repent
Jesus was sent
Forgiven, so we move on
Alpha and Omega

So, let us wallow in our own?
No. Rebuking from the throne
So that we all may benefit
How 'bout that?
Yes, the same He loves
Rebukes and chastens from above
The discipline of our Father
Repent and move on
The purpose of it all

Based on Revelation 3:19

No Serpent for Me

Asked according to my faith
Receive all that I prayed on
Remain strong
Spirit told me
God holds me
Ask, seek, knock
Father's blessings nonstop
Man's hearts filled with self
Bless our children that ask for help
How much greater is God in heaven
Ask for six—receive seven
I've seen these works
Faith, equal power God exerts
How must I ask, do I demand?
God answers to no man
Burdens to the throne
Step back, peace shown
Look not to men
Ask, seek, knock
Desires become possessions
No hesitation or questions
Father of great things

DR. CHARLES A. GUILFORD, III

Blessings from the King
Unto man as unto you
Perpetuate evil, and evil pursues
Listen, understand
It will be given—it will be found, and it will be opened
Praying and knowing
Light we all may see
God: "Ask and you shall receive"
According to our faith

Based on Matthew 7:7–12

Remaining the Same

Humble as a lamb
In the Will I stand
Word heard
Fear our God
No wrath
Mercy
My Father did not curse me
Blesses continually
Generations to come
Predestined my son
A humble path he shall walk
God's Word is more than talk
Way of life
Way to light
The proud fall every time
My pride not of His mind
True
The mighty removed from thrones
The humble replace them, and rule alone
Fear of God in their heart
New beginning and humble start
Blessings begin to flow

DR. CHARLES A. GUILFORD, III

Humble path I follow
Power of His arm
Removed pride-filled charm
Many speak and utter
Even rich, treat my brother
As my equal
Up with humble and lowly
Many walked before me
Those with humble hearts
Return to start
My life God please change
With riches and wealth, or linen of plain
Help your child to remain
Humble, the same

Based on Luke 1:50–53

The Healing of Sliders

God has seen the ways
Before steps were made
Is there healing ahead?
Mercy in His heart?
Our ways wrong
Will God carry us on?
Guidance bestowed?
Forced to carry the burdensome load?
God said, "Come to me"
Our sins seen
Healing for us
Resides in our trust
Belief and faith
God heals mistakes
Hearts true
Actions continue
"I will heal him of his backsliding"
Spoken by our Father indeed
He knows our needs
The wicked receive no rest
Wickedness dwells in their chest
So as troubled seas, casting up sin and tribulation

DR. CHARLES A. GUILFORD, III

No peace for a wicked nation
But the one who once was
Will always receive God's love
And will be healed if the doctor sees
Examples all over—me
Healed from the ways of the past
A backslider many times
God knew my heart and mind
My faith needed help
Healed me; harmed myself
Those near and far from the throne of grace
Return to their secret place
After backsliding into the ways of old
Ask, and God will heal your soul
Solid ground placed under the feet of the sliders
Our Father is waiting to heal

Based on Isaiah 57:18–21

The Second Delivery

How it could be?
Asked Jesus, how to be born again
Simply my Brother explained
The Spirit brings change
No one entered as flesh
A righteousness plate on his chest
He burns like the rest
Spirit not possessed
Born twice
Double life
Pushed from the womb
The other, our hearts consumed
Lesson Jesus taught Nicodemus
The rebirthed man
Flesh remains for a time
Spirit truly divine
Next to the Lord, my soul rests
Conceive in Spirit, pass away flesh
Spirit, heal me
Second delivery
Born again

Based on John 3:5–7

Thing Seeker

Before I could even blink
Worry
Storms came quick
God could not fix?
Cried out in doubt
My Father
Why bother?
Matthew 6:25–34
Worry no more
The things I need
God knew before me
He supplies my needs
Not my will
Yet still
First sign of drought
Heart doubts
God's mercy
He heard me
Faith was weak
Still gave food to eat
Many starve
Acquitted charge

JUST THINKING

Gentiles
Seek things, worry for long whiles
Solomon dressed no less than lilies
For me?
Will not worry about
God brings me out
Today enough for my heart
Tomorrow? When God allows the start
"Worry not, worry not," read words so clear
My Brother speaking to my heart, my Father to my ear
Worry not

Based on Matthew 6:25–34

This Morning

Before sunrise
God opened my eyes
Opened His book to Psalms
Told me of me
I was in need
Caused me to cry out
Heart doubts
Heard my call
Before I fall
Healed lying lips
Gave me a grip
My tongue
Warrior's arrows come
Coals from broom tree
Sin tried to consume me
Meshech and Kedar I dwelled
Destined for hell
Way too long
God says move on
One who hates peace
No place in me
Peace, not war

JUST THINKING

Enemy's work no more
Connected to *you*
Words remain true
Eyes to the hills
Help cometh for real
Heaven and Earth
My worth
Nothing on my own
Combined with God on the throne
My foot, not moved
Sin, not pursued
No slumber
God: marathon runner
He keeps
Can't sleep
Shade of right hand
His Word must stand
Sun never strikes by day
God's way
Moon hides at night
Never pursued by its light
Preserved from evil
His people
Out and in
Preserves all men
Chose His Will
My God is real
Forevermore

Based on Psalms 120–121

Timothy's Example

A word Timothy gave
Done throughout my days
Example for all to see
Older or younger than me
Fathers, mothers, sisters, and brothers
No matter my age, true to the word
Timothy, I surely heard
World can't dictate actions
God's word—ultimate passion
Spirit over flesh
Thank God
Let not my youth determine truth
Example to all
God won't let me fall
Timothy can help
Each scripture
More and more
Gift prophesied by old folks
No joke
Meditate
Future instructions
Study

JUST THINKING

Not only me He saved
Those passing my way
God's words
Timothy 1, I heard

Based on Timothy 1

Who Do We Call?

In times of struggle, who do we call?
Of our friends, who will always answer?
Question remains
Man's foolishness, death
Envy of his heart, his slayer
The calling of grace?
Or in time of struggle do we search for the secret place?
God has been and will be
So, in the struggle situations
Who do we call?
Foolish settle down in cursed residence
Offspring not safe
Gate is closed on their being
We have a source of protection
No deliverer; the foolishness
The hungry devour harvests
Think not twice about their possessions
Even their thorn resting food is consumed
Realization of affliction is that of truth
From the dust it doesn't rise
The ground doesn't cause trouble
But with this conception, it becomes double

JUST THINKING

And time continues to press on
So, who do we call?
Answer revealed
Few words
Continually heard
Each prayer we utter
Warning from a brother
Sparks fly
God in our hearts and on high
Pulling down of strongholds
He answers always
In the time of Job and forevermore
Yes, call!
From now until eternity
My Father answers the call of his child
Victim of his own will
For all that is endured, planned for sure
Answer to the question
Who do we call?

Based on Job 5:1–7

AUTHOR BIO

Dr. Charles A. Guilford, III is an educator with over twenty years of experience. His spiritual journey is encompassed in his passion for learning and teaching. His personal and professional experiences have fostered his desire to enhance the lives of others.

Dr. Guilford holds a B.A. in English from the University of Maryland Eastern Shore, an M.A. in the Art of Teaching from Bowie State University, and a Doctorate in Educational Leadership from Delaware State University. He is a published author, accomplished presenter, program developer, and evaluator, as well as a relied upon mentor and advisor for many in the national and international educational field.

www.ingramcontent.com/pod-product-compliance
Lightning Source LLC
Chambersburg PA
CBHW020530080526
44583CB00013B/811